# Getting and Keeping Your Mate "Trained," "Whipped," "Faithful," and on a "Leash!!"

A Personal Guide on
Fidelity and Relationships
in the '90s and the Year 2000

by
Brittian Wilder III

Gallery Publishing

Copyright © 1997 by Brittian Wilder III.

All rights reserved. No part of this book may be reproduced or transmitted in any form or by any means, electronic or mechanical, including photocopying, recording, or by any information storage and retrieval system, without the written permission of the authors, except where permitted by law.

Library of Congress Cataloging-in-Publications Data

Getting andkeeping your mate "trained," "whipped," "faithful," and on a "leash!!": a personal guide on Fidelity and Relationships in the '90s and the Year 2000 / by Brittian Wilder III.

ISBN 0-9662124-1-X

97-94926
CIP

Manufactured in the United States of America.

# DEDICATION

Special thanks to the disc jockeys and program directors around the country who made the surveys possible.

Special thanks and dedication go to the hundreds and thousands of people all around the world whose honest input made this three-year project a reality!

*This book was written to withstand the test of time. It is my "legacy" to you and to the development and inspiration of generations to follow.*

Keep this book in your family always!

*Brittian Wilder*

# Contents

Acknowledgments ................................................................. ix
Dedication from the Artist .................................................... xi
Introduction ........................................................................ 1
**CHAPTER I:** For Women Only (Finding Your Soul Mate) ........... 3
   Dating in the '90s—A Modern Day Game Show ..................... 3
   The Dating Game ................................................................. 6
   Is There Such a Thing as True Love? Is it "Gone with the Wind?"
      How to Know It, If You Truly Have it! ............................. 11
   Where to Find a Good Man ................................................. 14
   Is "Chivalry" Dead? In a Coma?
      Or Just Needs to Be Resurrected? ................................... 18
   Why Single Men Would Rather Stay Home than Date ............. 20
   Choosing a Husband ........................................................... 22
   How to Tell If Your Mate Is "Mom" Material ....................... 26
   What Makes a Man Fall in Love ........................................... 29
   Breaking down Your Mate's Defenses ................................... 33
   How to Get Your Man to the Altar
      Quick, Fast, and in a Hurry ............................................. 34
   "Turn Me On—Make Me Laugh" ....................................... 37
   How to Be a Sex Symbol past "50" . . .
      The New Sex Symbols of the '90s . . . Women 40–50! ....... 38
   How to Marry a Mate with Money ....................................... 41
   How to Tell by a Man's Butt Whether He Has $$$ .................. 44
   How to Put a Man on "Layaway"
      with a "Coochie Coupon" (or an IOU for Sex) ................. 47
   I Want Your Body!!! ............................................................ 51
   The Time to Use Sex as a Weapon ....................................... 55
   The 25 Most Guarded Secrets
      Men Never Want Women to Know ................................. 58

Can a Man Kick a Woman to the Curb Who's Great in Bed? ...... 62
Do Men Really Trust Women? ...... 64
Can Your Love Withstand the Rain,
   the Hurricane, Tornado, and Blizzard? ...... 66
Why the Bad Girls Are Getting All the Good Men ...... 68
Fattening up a Frog for a Snake ...... 70
Tips for All the Good Girls
   Who Always Seem to Pick Bad Men! ...... 73
Tips for Being in Love with a Mate That You Can't Stand! ...... 76
You Can Dress Him up
   but You Can't Take Him to the White House ...... 77
How to Have a "Happy Meal" When You Bring Home More
   Bacon and Your Husband—A Few Beans ...... 79
Choosing Between My Two Favorite Girls—
   My Mate and My Mother—Whom Would You Choose? ...... 81
The Ten Cities Where 65%
   of Married Spouses Cheat the Most ...... 83
How to Tell If Your Mate Is "Cheating"
   or an Out-of-Control Dog ...... 85
Why Men "Dog" Women ...... 87
The Most Popular Places Spouses Go to Cheat ...... 89
Overcoming an Abusive Relationship:
   "I Am Somebody and Deserve to Be Loved" ...... 91
How to Quench the Thirst for an Old Flame
   and Set Your Current Romance on Fire! ...... 92
How to Get a 50-Year Warranty with Your Marriage
   and a Maintenance Plan Free of Break up or Break down ...... 95
How to Keep Your Man at Home, Trained,
   Whipped, Faithful, and on a Leash ...... 101
How to Have the "Ultimate Orgasm" ...... 106
"Getting Your Freak on!" ...... 108
The "Wild Thing" Helper—What to Do When
   Getting "His" Freak on Is Turning "You" Off ...... 111

Breaking up Is Hard to Do, Scary to Do,
  and What Should You Do?............................................................ 113
What to Do When You Are Left
  Barefoot, Broke, and Pregnant .................................................. 116
Divorce! "Celebration" or "Sadness"
  Knowing When . . . The Time to Dissolve a Partnership........ 120
"Paying Rent On" or "Leasing" Your Lover!.................................. 122
"Playing it Hard . . ."
  How to Get Your "Macho Man" to Talk ................................. 124
Why the Beautiful Girls Are All Alone
  and "The Girl Next Door" Is Seldom at Home!...................... 126
Getting over a Broken Heart.......................................................... 127
Conclusion ..................................................................................... 132

**CHAPTER II:** For Men Only (Introduction)............................... 134
Running up the Price of "Coochie"
  The Price Tag for a Woman Has Gotten "Outrageous!"......... 139
How to Make Your Wife Your Girlfriend,
  the Other Woman, and Your Chick on the Side..................... 140
When a Woman Wants a Wedding Ring—
  She's Not "Above" Playing Dirty ............................................ 142
Is it Best to Tell Women the Unfiltered Truth? ........................... 144
All Kids Are Not like "Bey-Bey's" Kids . . .
  Dating a Woman with Children ............................................. 147
Staying in the "Game" . . . For All the Good Men
  Who Always Seem to Pick a "Bad" Woman........................... 152
"It's Crying Time Again"—and It's Very, Very Masculine ......... 154
Got to Have a Roughneck!............................................................ 155
Be Careful What You Ask for . . . You Might Get It! .................. 157
In the Dog House . . .
  Can a Woman Truly Forgive and Forget Infidelity? ............... 159

**CHAPTER III:** African-American Relationships ......................... 161
   Understanding a Black Man and Black Woman ......................... 161
   How Black Mothers Are Setting Their Daughters up
      for Bad Relationships .................................................................. 166
   Understanding a Black Man .......................................................... 169
   How Much Am I Worth as a Black Man? ..................................... 171
   Myths Black Men Believe about Black Women .......................... 173
   Appreciating a Black Man and Woman ........................................ 177
   Transforming an "Abused" Black Woman
      Back into a Loving Being ............................................................ 181
   We Both Wear the Pants . . .
      But Will the Real Men Please Stand up? ................................... 182
   Why the Available Black Men Are Excluding Black Women
      As "Ideal Mates" .......................................................................... 184
   Conclusion: The Truth Shall Set You Free ................................... 203
   My Beautiful Black Woman,
      There's Something You Should Know ...................................... 203

# Acknowledgments

You know, behind every successful author, there are people who also deserve praise:

To **God**, from whom "Inspiration" and "Greatness" come.

To **my family**, who stood by me and encouraged me through the perils and saga of my life. **Thomas L. Wilder, Sr., Amy Wilder, Thomas L. Wilder, Jr.**, his wife **Michell**, and my Uncle **Sammy Wilder** and Aunt **Emma Wilder**.

To **Robert Frank, Sylvia Williams** and **Doug Steele** of "Coast to Coast Top Twenty." Thank you for my first writing job.

To **Mike Roberts**, Program Director of V103, Atlanta, Georgia. Thanks for encouraging me not to waste my talent.

To **Hattie Dorsey**, Chairman of the National Coalition of the 100 Black Women. Thank you for your input into my project.

To **Tommy W. Dortch**. Thank you for your input and development of African-American men.

To **Amanda Davis**, anchorwoman, Atlanta, Georgia. Thank you for stopping what you were doing and "critiquing" my manuscript. Oh, yeah, many thanks for not "screaming" when you received my manuscript two days before deadline!

To **Gladys Knight**. I really appreciate you. Thank you for the interview—and I kept my promise by not telling anyone that we were alone in the bathroom. And, I never told anyone that you had short pants on and I was helping you roll your hair. I'll take our secret to the grave!

Thank you, **Carla Harper**, Editor of *Atlanta Metro* magazine for featuring my articles in your magazine.

Thanks a bunch, **Sheila Bronner** of *Upscale Magazine* for your encouraging words.

Thanks a lot, **Shirley Thompson**, in the medical profession, Atlanta, Georgia, for your input into my script and special motivation for me.

Many thanks go to **Don Spear**, author of the national best-seller, "In Search of Good Pussy." Thanks for your critique, encouragement and positive motivation for me.

Special thanks to **Stephanie Lymon**—your friendship through this project has been priceless.

Many thanks go to the legal expertise of: **Melody Y. Cherry, Forrest B. Johnson and Associates**, Atlanta, Georgia and **Frenonia Walls, Attorney at Law**, Detroit, Michigan.

# Dedication from the Artist

I would like to thank Almighty God for giving me the strength and talent to make an artistic contribution to this book. I also want to thank Mr. Wilder, a very talented writer and good friend: your encouragement has helped me a great deal (... you "know," Brittian). I could not have done this without the unconditional love and constant support of my family and friends; so I dedicate my contribution to them all: Mom, Dad, Yusef, and Hekima—I love you. "The branches of life span from the roots of family." Chrystale, Adrienne, Chandra, Althea, Todd, Bennie, Marcus, Meta, Angela, Tang, Jalal, Tiffany, Jasmine, Delandra, Karl, Ced, William, Roy, T-Rob, Lashonda, Toni, Snoop, Donna, Mann, Mee-Mee, Gino, Eddie, Nikki, Tay, Nickie, Don, Ian, Demetria, Asa, Ethel Wilson, Mr. and Mrs. Simms, Mr. and Mrs. Holloway, Mrs. Brown, Rev. Talley, Professor Dorsey, George Smith, all of Prairie View A&M University, my brothers in Christ, and N.E.W.U. . . . in no particular order because you've all played significantly important parts in my life. Your friendship has been invaluable. God bless you all.

*Imari*

# Introduction

Welcome to "Getting and Keeping Your Mate Trained, Whipped, Faithful, and on a Leash," a highly controversial and humorous self-help book that satirically traces the roots of relationships problems in the '90s and how to keep any mate *happy* and *committed*.

The book took three years to research and was created from the input and gripes of thousands of unhappy couples around the country.

Not only will you find a solution to your own relationship problems, but you will be able to "reprogram" your old ways of thinking as well as overcome all myths, stereotypes, doubts, and "hang-ups" you have about the opposite sex or race.

Now before we begin, let me first explain the terminology "trained, whipped, faithful, and on a leash":

To "train" means to "program" or "condition" your mate to be and do what you expect of them.

"Whipped" means to get your mate to a point at which they crave only *your* attention, affection, or intimacy.

"Faithful" is an undying devotion to you and to you only.

"On a leash" means to feel confident that your mate is happy and committed.

Now, why should we be concerned with getting and keeping our mates trained, whipped, faithful, and on a leash? Well . . . a national survey conducted in 1996 revealed that 65% of American spouses are "cheating";

68% of American spouses admitted they had "cheated"; and 58% of married spouses continue to cheat even after having been caught! (This survey was conducted by the author with the assistance of disc jockeys in all 50 states.)

According to a recent study done by Berkeley University, 50% of all marriages end in divorce. *The United States now leads the world in infidelity, divorces, and husbands divorcing spouses.*

A *USA Today* study revealed that white Americans have the highest divorce rate, while African-Americans have the highest divorce rate among minorities. Oriental, Asians, Latinos, Jews, and Italians have the largest infidelity and divorce rates and the highest commitment rates among other groups.

A 1990 Gallup Poll survey reveals 70% of American women believe that a diamond is a girl's best friend. But in a national survey conducted in 1996, it was discovered that 75% of American women now believe a good divorce lawyer is running "neck and neck" in terms of what a girl's best friend truly is. (Survey conducted by author.)

Now because men, women and some races differ in their needs and sexuality, I felt it necessary to set aside individual chapters just for this purpose.

Chapter I is designed to assist women in understanding the needs, sexuality, and thinking of men. Chapter I is labeled "For Women Only." Chapter II on the other hand, explores the needs, sexuality, and thinking of women and is labeled "For Men Only." Finally, Chapter III focuses entirely on, and explores, the sexuality, thinking, and needs of African-American men and women. Chapter III is labeled "African-American Relationships."

I have also provided real-life '90s relationship problems and wrote this book in everyday language so that each sex can get a first-hand view of what each experiences at the hand of the opposite sex.

As we explore relationships in the '90s and consider some helpful hints on keeping a mate *happy* and *committed*, you can decide for yourself, when all is said and done, whether your mate is truly a "dog" or just tired of being "dogged."

Shall we begin?

# CHAPTER I

## FOR WOMEN ONLY
## Finding Your Soul Mate

### Dating in the '90s—A Modern Day Game Show

Have you noticed that the moment you tell someone about a new love, the first question is always, "What does he or she do for a living?" As long as they have a good job and are getting paid, to your family or friends, they can do no wrong!

They could be "Dr. Jekyll and Mr. Hyde," or an axe murderer. But if you tell your mother they have a good job and want to marry you, your mother will probably say something like this: "Now, now, baby, so 'John' is a little possessive. It will change after the wedding. Look, baby, he's driving a 'Benz. He can't be all that bad!"

Or, he could be a "gorilla" disguised as a man and eat with his feet. Your mama will still find that "silver lining" even in his "cloud." "Baby, nobody's perfect! Look at his good qualities. He's a doctor; he has a big house!"

If you don't want him, give him two bananas for me. Teach him a few good table manners and tell him to call me in the morning. Or if a woman has it "going on," she, too, could be "off her rocker." In the '90s, it doesn't matter. It's the same thing. Your friends could tell you all day long, "Man, you better check out your girl. I heard she was the 'black widow' of New York City. Men have been disappearing all over the place, but dollar signs take over. Hey, man, forget what you heard. She is a CEO, drives a BMW and is 'fine.' At least when I go, I'll go with some 'fresh thread,' and not riding the bus—and with a big smile on my face."

If you are single or involved in a relationship or even married, this section was written especially for you. Before you get your emotions involved, pull your hair out, play with your emotions, here is an entire section dedicated to helping you make it over the "relationship hump."

*Passion*

## The Dating Game

You know, dating in the '90s has now become a "Modern Day Game Show," with everyone competing ferociously for that "right" man or woman. If you play the game well, then you get the person of your dreams. But if you play the game poorly, you sit at home alone and don't even get a consolation prize.

In the '90s, just like a game show, a man too must be screened before he qualifies for a date. This is done by asking various questions. Usually, these questions revolve around his job, his income, the type of car he drives, and what he can do to make you happy. Now, if you like his answers and his physique, then he wins the date. Oh, boy! So you go out with him, have a nice time, and before you know it, you're in love. Shortly afterwards, your phone stops ringing and your feelings and emotions get involved, and now you're playing the first game, called "Jeopardy!" Several days later, your mate calls you again and you soon find out they have lied and been unfaithful. It's time now for a game called "Let's Make A Deal!" It's usually played by saying, "Baby, I'm sorry, it won't happen again" or "Let's spend some time 'wining and dining' or going on some exotic vacation or wild 'shopping spree'." But during their absence, you meet "Larry." He is now putting pressure on you to make a choice. Your time is running out. The clock is ticking away! Should you keep your unfaithful lover or trade him in for Larry? Ah! Too late! You blew it! Larry goes off with someone else, and you're stuck with your unfaithful lover. Disgusted and frustrated with finding a monogamous relationship, you decide to throw caution to the wind and play the most popular game show of the '90s called "If the Price is Right." Now everyone has a price, and with some people it's an inexpensive dinner or a walk in the park. But with others, "It's both showcases, baby!" They want it all: money, trips, new cars, jewelry, and shopping sprees.

You're now dizzy and soon realize that all the "hoopla" isn't you. All you want is someone to love you unconditionally; and as fate would have it, "BAM!" You meet your "Mr. Right," and his name is "Joe." Now Joe doesn't have all the "flash," but he treats you well, and when you're together, nothing else seems to matter.

Excited, you bring Joe home to meet your parents. Your parents soon realize that he is not a doctor or lawyer, and now you're entering into a game called "Family Feud." You defend Joe by telling your parents that you love him. Your mother soon gets her turn and begins to play a game called "Wheel of Fortune." She slowly spells out the words she knows too well: P-O-V-E-R-T-Y . . . What is Poverty?!

After winning most of the rounds in the Family Feud, they finally give in and welcome Joe to the family. You are now happy because, for once in your life, you have found someone who loves you, *honors* you and *respects* you, and everything else is *just a consolation prize*!

It's funny when it comes to dating in the '90s—nobody is immune from a "broken heart" or getting caught up in "The Dating Game." That reminds me . . . not too long ago, I was working as a customer service rep for a well-known company in Atlanta, Georgia. You know, I really thought I was the man! Smooth talking . . . up on my game! And, above all, I could spot a heartbreak coming 100 miles away! Oh, yeah, I even ran the game a time or two. Remember, "All is fair in love and war" . . . but it's also true that "what goes around comes around." I soon found that out!

It was Saturday night, about 6:00. Man, was I excited. I'd finally gotten that date with Marsha. Marsha, Marsha, Marsha. She was 5'7", 130 pounds, an hour-glass figure, and an MBA in business. She was one of the hottest numbers in town—and she knew it. As I looked in the mirror, I slapped my favorite cologne on my face. Time was slipping away. Better get a move-on. Eight o'clock is almost here. What should I wear, what should I wear? Versace? Armani? Cerruti? Or JC Penney? JC Penney—no way! Marsha was definitely not a JC Penney girl. Decisions, decisions. Okay, Versace wins out! Where are my shoes? What did I do with them? Okay, Brittian, calm down, calm down. What time is it? 7:45. Okay. I'm about ready. Where are those Luther Vandross and Barry White CDs? Okay, it's all good. The "trap" is set. Marsha is not going to know what hit her! I'm the man! I'm the *man*! Buzz! Buzz! The alarm clock goes off—8:00 p.m. I made it, just in time. The doorbell should be ringing soon. Wait a minute. It's 8:15, 8:30. Maybe she had an accident. 8:45, now 9:00. Man, she stood me up. Man, I've been played! Let me call her at home . . . answering machine

... nobody's there. Man, I'm drained. I'll just call it a night!

The next morning I arrived at the office at 9:00, and it seemed I was the office joke! The fellas had seen Marsha out at a local hotspot with Kenneth Williams—the up-and-coming surgeon in Atlanta.

Later she "coldly" told me the reason she stood me up—it was that she had gotten a better offer. You see, I made only about $20,000 a year, and the only thing a brother who's making $20,000 a year could do for her was to tell her where she could find a man making $100,000 a year or better. To add insult to injury, she then looked at me, rolled her eyes, and said, "Brittian, you're not on my level. You see, I'm a manager, and you're only a customer service rep. It just wouldn't work. What would my friends say? What would the other managers think? I must admit, you *are* cute," she went on, "and fun to be with and talk a lot of 'jive,' but you know what's worse than a jive-talking man?"

"What, Marsha?"

"A jive-talking man with no money! And a wanna-be player, a hustler who's on a budget! Brittian, has it ever occurred to you I might not be the right one for you? Look at me. Do I look like a 'Payless' or 'Pick-a-Pair' girl? Do I look like a girl who dines at 'Hoochie Burger?' And I know I don't look like a girl who would ride in a Pinto without tinted windows! You see, I'm used to traveling first class, not coach. Trust me—to get next to me, a man knows that he better make sure I'm a 'frequent flyer.' In fact, I've been around the world so many times, I probably have stock in most airlines," she said, and laughed.

"Okay, Marsha, that's cool," I replied. "Since you think you're all of that ... if you do decide to start your own airline, I have the perfect slogan for you: *'We make you feel like you never left the ground—because we treat you like dirt!'*"

"Real cute, Brittian, real cute, you fake Donald Trump. I'm flattered that you find me attractive, but I'll be honest with you: I want to live the 'lifestyle' of the 'Rich and Famous,' not the 'broke and unknown.' I have champagne wishes and caviar dreams, not MD 20-20 wishes and pig's feet dreams. I know you like my style. But you certainly can't put class on layaway or afford this 'Rolls Royce,' especially on your 'Pinto' salary. I like my men to have the three 'B's."

*Marsha, Marsha, Marsha*

"The three 'B's,' Marsha?" I asked.

"Yes, the three 'B's' ... *bank, business,* or a *'Benz*. Now, Brittian, you also have the *three 'B's, but the wrong 'B's. You are broke, you are from 'Bama, and you just got busted!*" Marsha continued more softly. "Sweetheart, I'm not trying to hurt your feelings; it's nothing personal. But dating in the '90s is about business! And my 'stuff' is big business! It's Wall Street. It's a merger ... blue chip stock or a 'hostile takeover.' In fact, 'Barbarians' are at my gate as we speak. And, judging by my bank account, wardrobe, and pieces of fine jewelry, my 'stuff' continues to trade at an all-time high. So, my little 'chocolate friend,' until you're ready and able to run with the big dogs, why don't you just stay on the porch and bark? Bye, now, you cute little Chihuahua! Woof-woof! Talk to you when I return from Jamaica!" She walked away laughing.

With these words, my heart hit the floor. I was stunned. Is it like that in the '90s? Well, a few weeks later, whether it was fate or poetic justice, the word around town was that Marsha's doctor boyfriend had dropped *her* because, as he put it, she wasn't on his level, and she didn't make enough money! Man, there *is* a God! Shortly afterwards, as fate would have it, I was at a black art show at Piedmont Park in Atlanta, and I met a knockout attorney named Marilyn. We began to admire a piece of art by Imari (the illustrator of this book). We both smiled at each other, and a special chemistry passed between us. "You can have it," she said. "No," I replied, "You were here first."

We went back and forth, and finally she agreed to buy it. I asked her out for dinner that night, and she accepted. Marsha was old news, and Marilyn was number one—with a bullet!

During dinner that night, Marilyn made a 360° turn on me, and she too soon started to go down in flames. You see, all she talked about during dinner were her degrees, getting paid, and then she began to "cross-examine" me, trying to figure out how much money I made. Ah, man, another bourgeois, materialistic woman of the '90s. Ph.D., M.D., J.D.—are there any women left minoring in L-O-V-E? With Marilyn, I came to the conclusion that there is no shortage of good men, but there *is* a shortage of Mercedes-driving, $100,000-a-year making, briefcase-carrying businessmen or millionaires to go around. A woman might have a Ph.D., M.D., or J.D., but if she can't be "real," she will find herself very, very lonely.

## Is There Such a Thing as True Love?
## Is it "Gone with the Wind?"
## How to Know It, If You Truly Have it!

Whatever happened to men like Billy Dee Williams? You remember Billy Dee, "Mr. Suave and Debonair" from the movie, "Mahogany?" In the movie, Billy Dee had to "check" Diana Ross by telling her, "Success means nothing without someone to share it with..." Or what about Rhett Butler, the southern gentleman who gave up fame and fortune for Scarlett O'Hara in the movie classic, "Gone With The Wind?" And who can forget perhaps the greatest love story of them all, "Romeo and Juliet?" The two lovers would rather be together in death than to live apart in life. Wow! How could someone love another person that much? Do these kinds of men and relationships still exist? Are they gone with the wind? I must admit, true love still exists in the '90s.

You know you have found "true love" if your mate can stand the "rain," the bad times, the uncertain times, the times when the money is "low" and the bills are "high."

You know you have found true love when you will happily "catch" and share a cold from kissing the other person; when you know what each other is thinking without saying a word. You can look into your mate's eyes and receive the strength to fight Mike Tyson, slap King Kong, make "hopelessness" become "hopefulness," make you act silly, turn anger into a smile, make you want to give them your overcoat in zero-degree weather. He is no longer just a lover but also a friend, your hope, inspiration, a blessing, a miracle, a life-line, a four-leaf clover, a lighthouse in a rocky storm! You pray together, stay together, and fight together. He arouses you emotionally, spiritually, and physically. He makes you want to grab him, jump on him, kiss him, hug him, scream for help, dial 9-1-1, 9-1-2, 9-1-3, and even call the fire department or "Smoky the Bear" with a water pistol! He makes you feel alive. He makes you feel "Bold and Beautiful," "Young and Restless." You want to dance to the "Edge of Night" and have all his children in "General Hospital." You don't care what happens "As the World Turns" because in his eyes, you see "A Guiding Light." Even when it's cloudy outside, you want to "holler" like Tarzan or scream like James Brown—Ow-w-w-w! "I Feel Good!" And when you are out with him, you want to kiss him passionately. As you get older, and reminisce over the "Days of Your Lives," he is no longer just your lover, but your best friend, and one of the girls. If this is your mate, my independent woman of the '90s, then you have truly found your Billy Dee Williams or Clark Gable.

And if you are worried about what your family or friends think, "Frankly, my dear, I don't give a damn!"

*The Dance*

## Where to Find a Good Man

So . . . you're a "nice" girl, secure within yourself, couldn't care less about the "hoopla," the "glitz and glitter," or what someone else has. All you want to know is, where can you find a nice man, a person who is "God fearing," someone who will do "right," who thinks "us" rather than "me," a person who doesn't want you just for your money or your body. Where can you find someone who will work, cook dinner, be your buddy, lover, and "exotic fantasy," but also someone you can dress up and take to the White House or take home to meet "mom?"

According to a study done by *Cosmopolitan* or *Ebony* magazines, there are still good men available in the '90s. In fact, they are in every city and on every street corner (please don't overlook the laborers and blue collar workers, the skilled and the unskilled).

The locations known for the most single men are:

| New York | Miami | New Orleans |
| Los Angeles | Alaska | Memphis |
| Atlanta | St. Louis | Nashville |
| Washington, D.C. | Cleveland | Houston |
| Chicago | Dallas | Detroit |

If you just happen to live in one of these places, or any other place, and want to know, "Where can I find these single men?" try these places:

1. *At Church.* You've heard it once, and I've said it again and again—church is a good place to start seeking "Mr. Right." Join a singles ministry. Get to know the minister. Let him know you are available. In fact, it has been proven that relationships that started off at church usually can pass the test of time and become a "marriage made in heaven."

2. *At a Health Spa.* The men of the '90s are not only "money" conscious, but even more health conscious. While you are getting or keeping your body in tip-top shape, "work-it baby" shape, don't forget to check out the "action" around you.

3. *At the Grocery Store.* If you see a potential "victim"—excuse me—mate (chuckle), don't be afraid to introduce yourself to him or her. You can usually tell whether or not they are single by checking their shopping basket. Light shopping or TV dinners usually mean, "Baby, I'm single!" Also, check out their hands on the sly for a wedding band or wedding ring. If they are being "slick" and have taken it off for a little side action, you will see the tan mark left by the ring!

4. *At the Mall.* Don't be afraid to walk over to someone and start a conversation, because you are in a public and open area. The person should feel a little less threatened by you. If you see someone who looks appealing, don't let them get away. The worst thing in the world is, "I should have, could have, would have." Be bold! Be bad! You're a woman of the '90s, and it's your world. Forget about being a "nice" girl"—that's for wimps! It's a "love jungle" out there! You're on the prowl—Gr-rr-rr! If Jane can't keep Tarzan on a leash, she better keep him in the treehouse with Cheetah riding "shotgun"—Grrr!

5. *Join Singles Clubs, Social Clubs, or Dating Services.* Don't be embarrassed. Just because you don't have a man is no reflection on you. You haven't found the "right one," and you're not settling for a "minnow"—you're waiting for "Jaws!" Usually your friends know your taste in men. Don't be afraid to ask your girlfriend to hook you up.

6. *At the Park, Art Shows.* Outdoor concerts, flower shows, art museums, theaters and plays—these are all excellent venues for meeting new people.

7. *Happy Hour at Night Clubs.* Everybody says, "You can't find a good man at a bar." But during happy hour, this is where the available men congregate.

8. *Riding the Subway.* Many professionals and non-professionals alike are riding the subways. Don't be afraid to sit by a potential "victim"—sorry—mate—another "slip of the pen!" (chuckle).

9. *At Work.* Now this is good and bad. Your nice approach could be misinterpreted as "sexual harassment," so be very careful, especially if you're in a supervisory position. If you let a person know that you would like to date him, and the person says "no," let "no" mean "no." If you pursue it after that, things could get real "hairy."

10. *Social Functions, Fund Raising, Political Events, etc.* You'll find a lot of young professionals taking part in these types of affairs.

11. *Take Out a Personal Ad.* Don't be afraid to take out a personal ad in a local paper. It's the '90s, after all. Everybody's doing it. Make sure you meet your caller on your initial date in a public place, then take it from there!

12. *On the Internet.* Don't be afraid to put a little "love note" to a potential subscriber. Once you get a response, meet the person in a public place until you feel comfortable with them.

13. *At the Laundromat.* Make sure you check out the weekend action.

14. *In the Lobby of a Fortune 500 Company.*

15. *At a Wedding.* Remember, the groom has buddies.

16. *At a Cook-out.*

17. *At an Airport.* Hang out there when you have nothing to do and check out the action.

18. *On a Cruise Designed for single People.*

19. *Referral from a Mutual Friend.*

20. *At the Beach or at a Pool Party.* What you see is truly what you get!

# Is "Chivalry" Dead?
# In a Coma?
# Or Just Needs to Be Resurrected?

Do you remember the time when the "brave knight" risked his life to rescue the "damsel in distress," or the cowboy who jumped in front of a bullet to rescue his "love" and died in her arms with one single kiss from her lips? Or a time when the "good guy" actually got the girl, and together they would "ride off into the sunset?" When it came to "modern romance," the man would pick out a single rose for the lady, pull a chair from the table, or open the car door. Whatever happened to those times? Is "chivalry" dead in the '90s? If so, how can we resurrect it?

The problem in the '90s is that before the "women's liberation movement," women were perceived as helpless and defenseless beings who needed a big, strong man to protect and take care of them. Now these same women are making their own money, have their own homes and cars, and—if the truth be known—some of them are taking care of their big, strong men. Another problem lies in the popular TV shows, songs, and "rap" videos that we see. The record companies and networks are making billions of dollars every year exploiting and degrading women. Is "chivalry" dead, or "gone with the wind?" No, not really! But, I must admit, it is going to take a little work to bring it out of its "coma." Parents could have the biggest part to play in returning society to the time of "gallantry."

Mothers should once again teach their daughters what is "proper" and "ladylike." Fathers should once again teach their sons to respect women with words and deeds.

Now, let's take a "pop quiz" to see whether chivalry is dead in your personal relationship, or whether it's in a "coma," or simply needs to be resurrected.

1. Your mate still notices you. He quickly notices a new dress, new perfume, a new hairstyle, or whether or not something is bothering you.

2. He takes an interest in your day, or he's never too busy to see what is going on in your life.

3. He still remembers special occasions: birthdays, anniversaries, and promises.

4. He sends you flowers, love notes, and still flirts with you or still looks at you with "naughty" glances.

5. He respects your opinion and decisions.

6. He cooks you dinner, runs your bath water, or rubs your feet or back after you've had a hard day's work.

7. He still opens the door for you or pulls your chair out for dinner.

8. He's not too proud to apologize when he's wrong or keeps cool during a heated argument.

9. He refers to you by your "pet" name and frequently calls you "sweetheart, darling, love, or beautiful."

10. If someone is verbally or physically challenging you, you know he has "your back."

## Why Single Men Would Rather Stay Home than Date

You know, dating used to be an exciting time for most single men. Just the thought of going out with someone new was enough to motivate him to work hard all week, get a fresh haircut, buy a new suit or outfit, wash his car, and practice complimenting her in the mirror while he slaps on his favorite cologne.

According to a poll done among single men in a five-city survey (Los Angeles, New York, Boston, Kansas City, and Jackson, Mississippi), dating in the '90s is just not what it used to be. In fact, 47% of the single men interviewed said that they would rather stay home and watch TV than date. Here are the most frequently given reasons why:

1. It's too expensive. Depending on where you live, a casual date for two with dinner, dancing or a movie can cost from $75–$150.

2. Everyone is looking for someone else to make them happy instead of making themselves happy first.

3. Unrealistic expectations from women. Women want to be "wined and dined" in style, but they don't want to reciprocate.

4. Insecure about passing a woman's checklist: income, physical attractiveness, and social status.

5. Unappreciative—women can't appreciate the little or simple things.

6. Women play too many games and are too materialistic.

7. I'm waiting on God to send me my mate.

8. A lot of "quantity" but very little "quality."

9. I am too much of a "nice guy," and I don't want to be taken advantage of.

10. Too many diseases out there!

## Choosing a Husband

Now, to keep your marriage from becoming another divorce, there are certain "nevers" you should abide by:

1. *Never marry for money or financial security!* Ouch! Did I lose anybody on this one? Forget the saying, "What's love got to do with it?" Love has everything to do with a lasting relationship. In the game of life, money will come and go. Do you want your relationship or marriage to fluctuate with the stock market? Forget your mother telling you that it's just as easy to marry a rich man as it is a poor man. Let me examine this saying. Let's see. There are about 220 million people in America, and out of that 220 million, only 2% are millionaires. So the moral to this story is, "You better learn to love a poor man!"

2. *Never be so in love that you are blind.* Sometimes you may be in love with someone or want them so badly that you can't see that they are in love with what you have, who you are, and the lifestyle you represent.

3. *Never let your biological clock cause you to go "coo-coo" or do anything "coo-coo!"* "I'll take care of you. I'm young, single, available, and working. Let's get married. I need you to 'stabilize' me or help me grow up. I want to have kids before I'm 35. You're a man, I'm a woman, do your job!"

4. *Never let "hot sex" choose a wife or husband for you.* You can't "make love" for the rest of your life. I must admit, many have tried. Remember, you've got to have a couple of dollars to pay the rental company to pay for the bed that you are making love on.

5. *Never be totally dependent on a man!* Did I lose any friends on this one? Is everybody still in the Amen corner? Even if you are a housewife and your man treats you like a queen, have a degree or a skill or something to fall back on. People have a tendency to respect you more and value you more when they know you don't have to put up with foolishness. For example, how many times have we seen or heard of a woman being abused, and the first thing we think is, "Why doesn't she leave?" Her answer is, "With what? Go where? Driving what? Work where?" She is totally dependent on him. She has no education, no money, no skills and, oftentimes, no friends.

6. *Never make a man your life—make him part of your life!* Show your man a lot of attention, but don't smother him. If a man is your entire life, suppose he dies. What will happen to you and the kids?

7. *Keep your family and your mother out of your business.* Lord, if you ever want your marriage to dissolve, let your family or your mother put their nose or two cents' worth into your business. "Baby, I knew he wasn't any good and couldn't keep a job. I knew his daddy when he was hustling peanuts in front of the dollar store—he wouldn't work either." Or, "Son, your wife gets her 'low-down' ways from her mama. Her entire family has a 'mean streak' in them. You're better off without her."

8. *Make your mate feel needed and include them in all aspects of your life.* Whether you are rich and have been advised to make a worldly decision, ask your mate, "Baby, what do you think?" whether or not they know the answer is immaterial. It's always nice to ask.

9. *Regardless of how busy you are, always take time to notice your mate.* From the smell of her favorite perfume to when she buys a new dress or how she acts when something is on her mind. Remember birthdays, watch a game on TV with your man. Go outside to play ball with him or help him wash the car. Notice his cologne or give it to him when he's looking good.

10. *You can't change someone once you are married.* They must want to change and strive to do so before the wedding.

11. *Never belittle your mate's work.* If he or she sits at home with the kids, don't take the attitude of "what kind of stress are **you** under? The only thing you do is sit at home all day." Have you ever babysat one, two or three kids and tried to keep the house clean? Have you experienced the demands of being a mother? It's a 24/7 job, with little pay and sometimes little appreciation. You are always working overtime without overtime pay.

12. *Spend some quality time together.* Even if it's nothing more than talking while you wash the dishes together. Go to a movie, walk or jog around the neighborhood together. You *must* take time to have an "affair" with your mate.

13. *Always let them know your true feelings or opinions about an issue—up front.* Don't let weeks pass, then finally explode, pull their cards and read them. This would certainly put distance in your relationship.

14. *When you are going through family problems, get the kids, before anyone goes to bed, and bow down on your knees as a family and pray together!* The Bible teaches that when two or more gather in His Name, or ask in His Name, it shall be granted!

15. *You can't have any secrets!* When they are discovered, trust goes out the window. For example, if you have kids, girlfriends, bank accounts, or residences outside your relationship.

Now that you know what to look for when choosing a mate, let's see if we can get your soul mate to fall in love.

## How to Tell If Your Mate Is "Mom" Material

Once you find your soul mate, the most important person you want to impress is your mother. Now both single men and women agree that there are usually two kinds of mates you will encounter when searching for your soul mate:

#1. The kind of mate you bring home to meet your mother,

and

#2. The kind of mate you bring home to meet your mother . . . when you know your mother is not going to be there.

The "million dollar question" is, how do you know which one you have?

A woman knows her mate is "mom" material if:

1. *He believes in God or a higher power.* Sometimes life is going to throw you a curve where prayer, faith, hope, and courage are the only things that will get you through. If your mate has a firm base in faith, they will be able to make it through those difficult times.

2. *He's not known north, south, east, and west of your city.* Nobody wants a mate who's been with every other woman in town, especially with so many diseases floating around. And every woman wants to feel her man belongs only to her.

3. *He's employed, has a stable residence, and a telephone number.* Usually if someone doesn't have a stable address or telephone number, they are running, hiding, or—far worse—into something illegal.

4. *His smile is not 14k gold top to bottom.* Well, we won't even go there . . . you know the answer to this one.

5. *He hugs her instead of hits her during a heated argument.* If you really want to see whether your mate is abusive, see how they react during an argument. Usually what someone thinks of you is when their true colors come out. If they can't control themselves, then they are not for you.

6. *He spends his money wisely.* Good spending habits are important in building your financial future. The less time you are arguing over money, the more time you can spend making it.

7. *He doesn't drink excessively or use drugs.* It's self-explanatory. Save yourself the heartache.

8. *He respects her opinion and can accept constructive criticism.* Since a relationship involves both people, your contribution and how you feel is equally important. Everyone should be able to accept constructive criticism, especially from someone who genuinely cares about them.

9. *He wants to get inside her head and heart instead of her bedroom.* Lovemaking is important in a healthy relationship, but it becomes even more exciting when a man makes love to your mind and heart first.

10. *He wants a monogamous relationship and a family.* Nobody wants to waste their time. The days of "fun and games" are over.

Now a man also wants to know if a woman is "mom" material. To a man, a woman is "mom" material if:

1. *She runs "toward" him when there is trouble and not "away" from him.*

2. *She's part of the solution and not part of the problem.*

3. *She gives back to the community.*

4. *Her true beauty is not "outward" but "inward."*

5. *She loves him half as much as his mother loves him.*

6. *She knows what he is thinking by one single glance.*

7. *She will gladly share his cold because she can't keep her lips off him.*

8. *He always knows where to find her.*

9. *She always tells him the truth, even when a lie would make him feel better.*

10. *She is dedicated and dependable.*

## What Makes a Man Fall in Love

What makes a man fall in love is perhaps the 8th wonder of the world. To truly give an answer a woman can "sink her teeth into," I decided to present this complex question to 1,000 single men across the country. Here are the most often repeated answers they gave:

1. *A woman who is appreciative.* According to single men, before they will put up with a selfish woman, they would rather be by themselves, eat by themselves, and sleep by themselves.

2. *A woman who constantly asks him "What can I do to make you happy?"* Out of the 1,500 men surveyed, only 287 have actually had their mates ask them that question.

3. *A woman who supports him emotionally.* Every day men hear what they are not. A woman who reinforces what he **is** is priceless.

4. *A woman who shows him a lot of attention.* Men are just like children . . . they, too, must be pampered.

5. *A woman who brags to her friends about him.*

6. *A woman who thinks he is smart.*

7. *A woman who asks his opinion about different subjects, regardless of how trivial.*

8. *A woman who couldn't care less what her friends or parents think of him.*

9. *A woman who sits quietly and listens to him.*

10. *A woman who reinforces his positive attributes and "harps" less on the negatives.*

11. *A woman who gives him "space" or "cave" time.* If a woman doesn't allow a man space, or "cave" time (a time to be alone), then she will push him away or push him into the arms of another woman.

12. *A woman who lets him know that she is interested.* But she continues to make herself a challenge to him.

13. *A woman who is there when he needs her . . . and checks on him to make sure he is okay.*

14. *A woman who kisses him when he's upset or angry.* Remember, it takes two to argue.

15. *A woman who tries to become his version of the perfect woman.* Now many of you are saying that a man should accept the woman for who she is. Well, this is true, too, but until the woman gets him to the altar, the motto is, "Whatever is clever."

16. *A woman who is adventurous, spontaneous, and "naughty."*

17. *A woman who feels that he comes before her career.* Again, very few men will ask a woman to give up her career for him. Still, a man would like to feel that his mate would gladly do it.

Among the other things that are "turn-ons" to men are:

18. *A beautiful smile.*

19. *A woman who smells nice.*

20. *A sexy dress.*

21. *A home-cooked meal.*

22. *A nicely toned and developed body.*

23. *Nice hair . . . whether it's long or short.*

24. *A nice back rub after work.*

25. *Nice eye-contact.*

26. *Reading him a poem in bed.*

27. *A woman who rents a sexy movie and then "recreates" those love scenes with him.*

28. *Calls him in the middle of the night just to say "I love you."*

29. *Asks him out to lunch and then lunch turns into his being tied to the bed and doing the "wild thing."*

30. *Buys some scented bubble bath and bathes him by candlelight.*

31. *A woman who shaves him in the morning.*

32. *A woman who gives him a private "striptease."*

33. *A woman who never "snoops" through his personal things.*

34. *Explores his body with her tongue and mouth.*

35. *Carries a picture of him in her wallet.*

36. *Makes a big fuss over him when he's sick or hurt.*

37. *Makes an "X" rated movie with him and frequently talks dirty to him during sex.*

38. *A woman who reads the paper with him.*

39. *A woman who listens to his dreams.*

40. *A woman who plays romantic music during dinner.*

41. *A woman who very seldom wears panties.*

42. *A woman who takes a bottle of champagne to bed.*

43. *A woman who works out with him.*

44. *A woman who dresses him when he's going to work and then undresses him when he returns.*

45. *Cuddling after lovemaking.*

46. *Buys a feather and uses it during foreplay.*

47. *Finds out his favorite love song and then sings it to him.*

48. *A woman who lights candles and serves wine with the simplest meal.*

49. *Occasionally tells her friends that she can't go out with them because she's with him and . . .*

50. *A woman who occasionally lets him dress her.*

## Breaking down Your Mate's Defenses

You know, we all have "hang-ups" that keep us from accepting love or being loved. But fortunately, "what is in a person's heart will eventually come out through their mouths and their actions."

To break down your mates defenses so that you can get next to his heart and soul will require a little work, time, and patience. So let's start the process right now.

The biggest complaint that American men have with their spouses is that they are "selfish" and "unappreciative." And I didn't realize how prevalent this was until I surveyed 1,500 men across the country.

Out of the 1,500 men who were interviewed, only 363 admitted that they've ever experienced their mate's telling them *they were appreciated.* And as I had mentioned earlier, only 287 men out of the 1,500 ever experienced their mates asking them what they can do to make them happy.

Well, to keep your mate out of the "complaint department," here's a little exercise I want you to try at least twice a week.

Call your mate unexpectedly at work and tell him, "I just called to tell you that I love you and appreciate you and from this day on, I am going to try to be the best thing that ever happened to you." If your mate is unavailable, leave the message with his secretary. Then ask the secretary to read it out loud the moment he is available. Think what kind of impact your thoughtfulness will have on your mate. And think of the respect and admiration others will have for him. Remember, we all have hang-ups, and it's comforting to know that someone "truly" cares about and appreciates us.

## How to Get Your Man to the Altar Quick, Fast, and in a Hurry

Despite popular belief, men, just like women, also dream about finding their soul mate. Let's face it: being single in the '90s is definitely not "all of that"—especially with so many diseases floating around. In survey after survey of single men around the world, 95% of these single men agreed that if they could find a woman with the "total package," they would have her at the altar *quick, fast, and in a hurry*!

1. *A woman who makes him feel that he's not missing anything* . . . most men feel that once they say "I do," they're done! If you are dreaming of wedding bells and having this problem with your mate, first find out what your man enjoyed most about being single, whether it was hanging out with the fellows or occasionally going out to clubs. Give him some rope. If he truly loves you, he won't "hang" himself.

2. *Don't become to accessible or too predictable.* Let your man know that you love him. But occasionally throw on that dress that got him "hooked" and go out alone or with the girls. Until that ring is on your finger, never become too predictable or too accessible.

3. *Compliment and notice him.* Just like you, men like to be noticed. Just in case you're not aware of if, men have large and fragile egos. If your man is looking good, "give it to him." Do you realize that men hear every day in the media someone telling him what he's not? Tell him that he's "all of that" and a "plate of grits on the side" (chuckle). See what happens!

4. *Be pleasant and be his best friend.* Are you frequently "checked" about your attitude? It's not what you say but *how* you say it. Be part of the solution and not part of the problem. The very worst way your man could describe your relationship is that he's in love with a woman he can't stand.

5. *Be a woman who loves her man half as much as his mother loves him.* His mother will accept his faults, habits, and "shortcomings." He can always depend on his mother. Regardless of what happens she always knows what to say. She will never leave him.

6. *Pamper your man and spoil him rotten!* Take him out to dinner occasionally. Give him a nice back rub when you are together. Always give him kisses and hugs when you see him. Send him little love notes at work and even flowers.

7. *Be a person with whom your man can be totally honest and who generally wants to make him happy.* The hardest thing for a man to do is to tell the "unfiltered" truth because he's afraid you may throw it up in his face the next time you are arguing. Tell your man that you genuinely want to make him happy. Better than that—SHOW HIM!

8. *Be a woman who can cook.* Face it, ladies, men still believe in a girl who can cook. So get to his heart through his stomach. But please—don't "microwave" a man to death!

9. *At work, you might be the boss, but at home, allow him to be the man.* This is also a big complaint men have with dating professional or "high-powered" women. You may give the orders at work, but at home allow him to be "king" and to take charge. He's not one of your employees or a staff member. He's your man! If you bring home more bacon, remember, it's all going in the same "frying pan."

10. *Continue to offer exciting and adventurous lovemaking. Always remember that making love to a man also begins "before" you enter the bedroom.*

## "Turn Me On—Make Me Laugh"

"Hey, man, I met this girl named Tracy. She is a high-powered lady, but she is naughty, spontaneous, and silly."

Now normally, when you hear someone describe someone else as "crazy," a lunatic, insane, silly, or "buck wild," you would think she is not the one. But to be honest, these adjectives are some of the highest compliments a man can pay a woman. And to be *perfectly* honest, there are three things a man never forgets: (1) a woman who makes him laugh, (2) a woman who treats him well, and (3) a woman who is great in bed!

In my surveys among men across the United States, the *biggest turn-off* is a woman who is "boring," "unexciting," or just plain "tired." Don't get me wrong: you don't have to tell a joke for your date every five minutes. But on a date, be charming and fun to be with. Remember, the purpose of a date is to get to know the person, relieve stress, and have fun. Dating should not be a "job" but an "adventure," something to look forward to. The worst thing you can be is a "tired," "uptight," "boring" date, talking only about your education, credentials, and material possessions.

You'll find that if you have *personality and charisma*, dating in the '90s will become very, very easy. But on the other hand, if your personality is bad and you are constantly turning off all of your friends, you can still get a woman or man with your "cash, business, or a 'Benz."

## How to Be a Sex Symbol past "50" . . .
## The New Sex Symbols of the '90s . . . Women 40–50!

A couple of years ago, I was working for a well-known company here in Atlanta, and one of the fondest memories of that company was about my supervisor, Ms. Cookman. She was between 40 and 50 years of age, had short, "feathered" hair with gray streaks; she had brown eyes, was 5'7", and had full lips. All the single men in the company had the same problem. We all had a "crush" on Ms. Cookman, and we all agreed that she was one of the sexiest women we had ever met. Now usually when a man describes a woman as "sexy," a person immediately begins to think of an "hour-glass" figure, long, slender legs and long, flowing hair. Those attributes make a woman sexy all right, but in the '90s, there is a new group of "sex symbols" on the horizon, and men everywhere are falling under their spell. The sex symbols are women between the ages of 40 and 50. Now let's take a look at the reasons men find these women "sexy" and "hot!"

1. Inwardly beautiful: True beauty and sexiness begin inwardly and radiate outward. This type of beauty makes a woman very, very sexy.

2. Elegance and sophistication: "Mature" women radiate class and style. It's in the way they walk, talk, dress, and carry themselves.

3. Meticulous concern with their personal appearance: Because they are "mature" women, extra care and pride is taken in their personal appearance, from their bodies, hair, skin, nails, feet, to the way they dress.

4. Secure within themselves: Usually they have their own careers and genuinely want to enhance their man and make him happy.

5. Personality: Nothing is more of a "turn-on" to a man than a big smile, a kind word, and a pleasing personality.

6. Experience: They know what "buttons" to push to bring out the best in their men.

7. Humorous: Laughter has always been an "aphrodisiac."

8. Adventurous: Because they have experienced life, they like to try and do different things, and to go to different places.

9. Pamper their men and cater to his ego: Men love to be spoiled rotten.

10. Bring out the "chivalry" in their men: Because they are usually from the "old school," your manners are constantly in "check," from pulling out their chair for dinner to opening doors.

So, to all the "Ms. Cookmans" everywhere, women between the ages of 40 and 50, the next time a young man tries to flirt with you or "give you the eye," laugh and take it all in stride—because he's just letting you know that you still "have it!"

*Breeze*

## How to Marry a Mate with Money

How many times have we heard someone say, "It's as easy to marry a rich man as it is a poor man" or "You don't need any help to starve to death" or "The only kinds of friends you need are 'green' ones?"

Let's face it—we all have fantasized about being rich—hitting the Lotto, the jackpot, living on "Easy Street," or telling the boss what he or she can do with that job. And when all else fails, we fantasize about marrying someone with money. At this point, the "million dollar question" is, *where* do I find a mate with money? And *how* do I get someone like that to fall in love with me?

First of all, before I even address those questions, let's "cool our jets" for a second, back up, and establish a "yardstick" with which we can measure what is bonafide "rich." Before you grab your "pick," "hard hat," and "shovel," you must believe that "there is gold in those hills"; then you won't be confused by "Fool's Gold": a fancy car whose owner has no money, no house, and is wearing a "Fakelex" instead of a Rolex.

"Materially rich" is someone who has at least $1 million or better in cash. With stocks and bonds, the situation fluctuates, sometimes radically. So the $1 million in cash will be our "yardstick" for measuring "rich."

To find a mate with money is quite simple. People with money frequent events and places where other moneyed people go—social events, political rallies, museums, plays, church, charitable events, volunteer work, and famous resorts. You see the names of these places all the time in the media where people are making charitable donations or spear-heading worthwhile causes.

According to *Forbes* magazine, the places with the most millionaires are:

1. California
2. New Hampshire
3. New York
4. Florida

5. Atlanta
6. Dallas
7. Houston

In fact, at this moment there are one million millionaires in the United States. Now that you know where the dollars are, how do you "go for the gold?" How do you find your "Sugar Daddy," a young "tenderoni" with fat pockets or a million-dollar entertainer, athlete, or businessman?

I have interviewed 100 men who are truly among the "bonafide rich"—$1 million or better in cash—ranging in ages from 21 to 60. I asked them point-blank what it would take for someone to "reel them in." This is the "game plan" they revealed that is requisite when you are "going for the gold":

1. *Appear to truly care about them and their well-being.* Some people with wealth are very distrusting of others. They realize everyone around them doesn't have their best interests at heart. If you are someone who truly and genuinely cares about them, then you are priceless.

2. *Be confident and secure when you meet them.* Don't be overwhelmed by them. They get this all the time. Pretend as though they are "plain Joe." Tiger who? Will who? People can't stand rejection, especially when they are supposed to be "all of that."

3. *Make them respect you from the start.* You are also a superstar! Never let anyone treat you like a "groupie" (someone who will do anything to be with them). If they are "out of line," "check" them.

4. *Have intelligence to go with beauty.* People who are rich or successful want someone whom they can dress up and take to the White House.

5. *Be a good listener.* Everyone loves someone who listens to them, and with whom they can honestly talk as well.

6. *Never be a "yes lady."* They have enough of them around.

7. *Have your own goals and dreams.* Strive to make your own story a success instead of always wanting to become part of theirs.

8. *Never ask them for anything.* If you follow helpful hints one through seven, they will offer it to you. They will recognize you as someone unique or out of the ordinary.

9. *Have a positive and pleasing personality.* You can catch more "flies" with honey than you can with vinegar!

10. *Be a woman in the "street" but an "adventure" in the bedroom.*

Bear in mind, however, that you may have already hit "pay dirt" or found your "Sugar Daddy," a young tenderoni with fat pockets. When you have someone who loves you, honors you, and treats you well, then you can proudly look at your "pick," "hard hat," and "shovel" and go into retirement because you have truly struck gold!

## How to Tell by a Man's Butt Whether He Has $$$

You know, while researching and writing this book, I thought I had heard everything. But while hanging out at local clubs in Detroit, Washington, D.C., Atlanta, and Los Angeles, women revealed to me that they can look at a man's butt and tell whether he actually has money!

Let's take a look at these "nice girls" in "action."

All the "butt" ladies in the house say, "Owwwww! Owwww! Work it, Baby! Work it! I wonder if he has a nice 'hot dog' to go with those 'buns'!" It's ladies' night out—you're a woman of the '90s. You're getting paid. You're proud! You see a "tight butt" and now you're on the "prowl!" Nice girls are for wimps! If "Jane" doesn't want "Tarzan" butt-pinched, she had better put a bigger "diaper" on him, keep him in the "treehouse," and make "Cheetah" ride shotgun!!!

If you're a lady of the '90s, and *one of your New Year's resolutions is you're "going for the gold,"* that is, looking for a man with money, grab your "hard hat" and put your "pick" and "shovel" on your back. According to 100 women interviewed in these cities, hitting the jackpot is not that difficult. You can easily tell whether a man's pocket is "fat" by checking out his "butt"—to see whether your "baby" has a "little back." According to our "booty experts" in these four cities:

1. If a man has "buns of steel," he might be loaded with "sex appeal" and have a "nice behind," but his pockets are "light" behind. You see, in order to keep his body (mainly, his "butt") in tip-top "work-it-baby" shape, a man has to spend hours in the gym working out and "loving himself" ... thus leaving little time to make the "big bucks!"

2. A "little butt," or one where you can see a "nice print" or "form," but nothing so tight that you can bounce a "brick" or quarter off ... then he's "up and coming"—he has to balance time between "work" and "working out!"

3. As the butt *decreases*, the men with the "real money" increase. *A flat behind means a man is sitting down making money on the telephone line!*

4. Zero butt or "sagging pants" means the man is "getting paid" and "bulging out" where it counts—in the back pocket.

5. Finally, Ching! Ching! Ching! According to the women in our four-city survey, *the men with the "big or flabby butts" are the "real deal Holyfield"*—you can rest assured they are not the "Section 8" minimum wage-earning, Jheri curl dripping, bus-catching, rent-flashing, weight-pumping men with a lot of *ass* and *very few assets*!

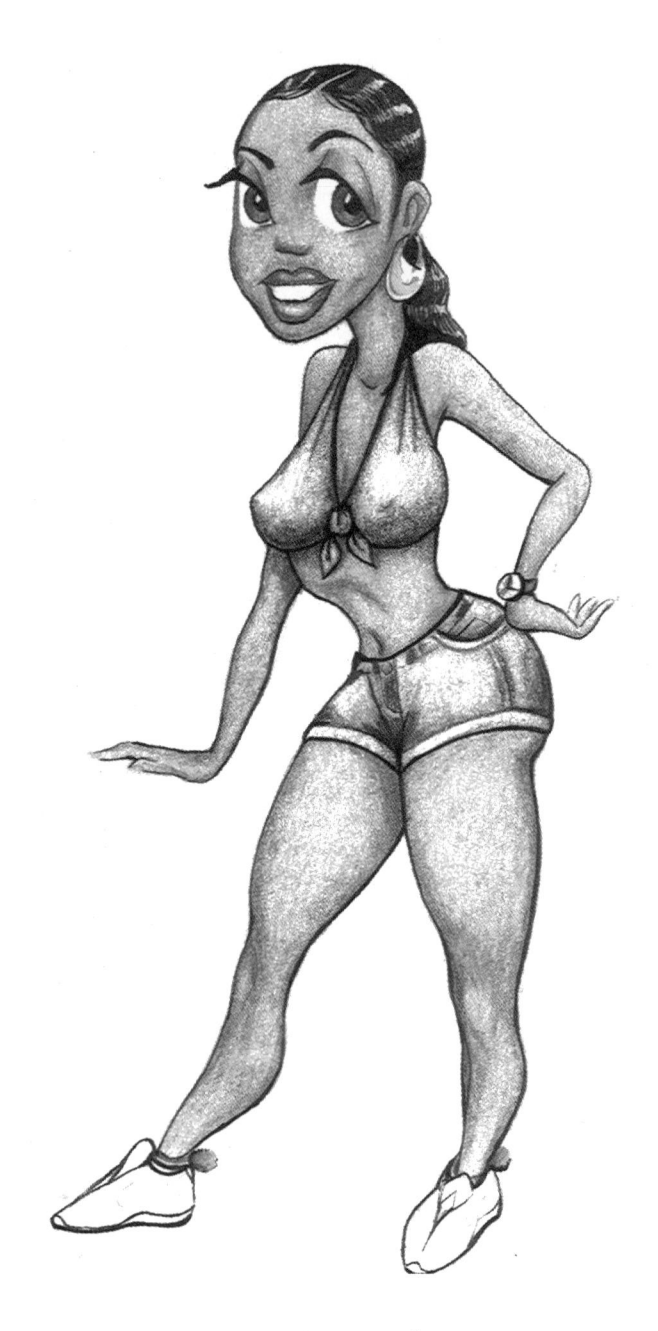

*I'm a Lady*

## How to Put a Man on "Layaway" with a "Coochie Coupon" (or an IOU for Sex)

In playing the dating game, you will encounter men who feel that once they "shell out" a few dollars for an expensive dinner or evening out, this is a guaranteed "IOU" for sex. And sometimes, you will encounter a man to whom you are so physically attracted that you'll want to rip his clothes off, then rip your clothes off, make the bed rock, even when you are "doing it" on the floor! But just when you are about to throw caution to the wind and answer that unmistakable "booty call," you remember that "good girl" stuff your mother used to tell you: "Good girls never 'do it' on the first date. Men respect women who make them wait, and don't give your 'stuff' away free!" If it's not your mother's voice "cockblocking" (preventing sex), then your own insecurities start to kick in: "The timing is not right, it's too soon, or I don't want this relationship to end up in just another fling, one-night stand, or two ships that pass in the night." So while you're running hot and cold, and your mate is totally confused and frustrated, all is not lost. Have your cake and eat it, too! Do the next best thing—give that man a "coochie coupon." A "coochie coupon" is basically an IOU for sex. Now, what's so nice about a "coochie coupon" is that you set the "expiration date" or "pay-off" date. The longer the man waits, the more interest your "coochie coupon" accumulates—and the more valuable it becomes. You can determine what value the "coochie coupon" entitles the holder to. For example, an expensive dinner will get the holder a hot, passionate kiss and a back rub. A movie entitles him to a passionate hug, and an inexpensive dinner doesn't entitle the holder to anything but talking dirty to him on the telephone.

No, you cannot find a "coochie coupon" in the Sunday paper or get one at your local grocery store. A "coochie coupon" is a figure of speech. This is how to put an oversexed man on "layaway" with a "coochie coupon":

> **Step #1:** First of all, tell him something like, "Baby, you know I really enjoy being with you, and no man has treated me so well—I feel as though I'm so special—you

take me out to expensive dinners, dancing, on vacation . . . that shows you have 'class' . . . and when the time is right, I will make you call '9-1-1, 9-1-2, 9-1-3' and 'Smoky the Bear' with a water pistol." At this moment, your mate feels that he's out of the ordinary and so special that he will chill for a minute. Now let's move on to step #2.

**Step #2:** Involves being very affectionate. Shower him with hugs, kisses and affection.

**Step #3:** Don't be overly impressed by material things like a nice car or house. You don't want him to feel as though he's "buying" you and getting a "sucker" free.

**Step #4:** Invite him over for dinner. Tell him what you want, your dreams, your ambition, what you want from him, from the relationship, and how he fits into your future.

**Step #5:** If he's still there and talking about making a commitment to you, let him know how you honestly feel about him.

**Step #6:** Let him know how you can enhance him. Tell him you will be an asset, not a liability.

**Step #7:** Dress sexy, but don't wear a dress so short that he thinks it's a "naughty top."

**Step #8:** Find out how he feels about kids.

**Step #9:** If he's still around after a "coochie coupon" (steps one through seven), and you feel he's your soul mate, clip his "coupon" and immediately replace it with:

**Step #10:** *A "coochie credit card"* with overdraft protection. From that point on, it's "open house" and everything is on sale!

*Her Curves*

## I Want Your Body!!!

... is perhaps the biggest thing to "keep on the look-out for" when playing the dating game. Let's face it. We all like a nice body, developed legs, bulging biceps, a nice chest, toned thighs, and a tight butt. In fact, in the '90s, the motto is "If you've got it, flaunt it," or if you don't have it, simply have it made with silicone or plastic! Women everywhere have told me they think Jean-Claude Van Damme (movie star and martial arts expert) has a nice, tight butt, while men secretly check out Janet Jackson's and Toni Braxton's "tush."

Most people will agree that, if you are going to sell a product, you must advertise it whenever possible. Well, that is somewhat true. A little advertising doesn't hurt the product, but you must be concerned with the product's image. You need to leave a little to the imagination for the "buyer" or "shopper." Too much advertising cheapens the product.

For example:

1. You know your jeans are too tight when you have to carry your driver's license in your mouth.

2. You know your jeans are too tight when you have to go to the bathroom with a "crew," a crowbar, and a couple of standbys.

3. You know your pants are too tight when you go to pick up $50 you see lying on the ground and a 75-year-old woman in a wheelchair three blocks down the street beats you to it.

4. You know your pants are too tight when you take them off, and there is a loud "pssss-ss-ss-ss" as you unfold on your bed like a blow-up raft.

5. You know your pants are too tight when you have to go on a diet to take them off.

6. You know your "Daisy Dukes" are too short when there isn't enough cloth to spell the words "Daisy Duke" on them, so you have to abbreviate "D.D."

7. You know your dress is too small when you find more cotton on a Q-Tip.

8. You know your dress is too tight when you normally wear a 32-B cup size and your breasts now look like 44-DD's.

9. You know your dress is too short when your three-year-old daughter is constantly asking you to please stop wearing her clothes.

10. You know your dress is too short when you bought it from Victoria's Secret or Frederick's of Hollywood and they are boycotting you.

Now that we know how to "dress for success" and not get an "arrest," how can a nice boy and girl tell *when someone wants only to get the milk without buying the cow!?!* Here are some dead-giveaways:

1. When you first meet them, they focus not on your eyes, but on your breasts or below the waist, and even talk to that part of your body.

2. They are constantly making lewd remarks like: "Your daddy must have been a brick mason to have stacks like that"; "Your lips are so big and juicy, you can French-kiss

a moose"; "Your butt is so big, if there was a fire and we had to 'haul ass,' you would have to return for a second trip"; or, "Baby, don't ever try to breast-feed a baby because that would be child abuse!"

3. If they are overly affectionate and can't keep their hands off you.

4. They tell you up front, boldly, "Baby, I want your body! You and me—the two of us, doing the 'wild thang'!"

The moral of the story is:

1. Too much advertising cheapens the product.

2. Why buy the cow when you can get the milk free?

and

3. Why pay full price (a commitment or a wedding ring) when you can "catch a sale," put it on layaway, rent to own, or lease with an option to buy?

*Sex as a Weapon*

## The Time to Use Sex as a Weapon

To get your mate to "open up" and find out what they honestly think of you will often require drastic action. You see, men have been programmed to "hold back." Men use the words "I love you" to get sex, and women use sex hoping that it will get them love.

Now with some mates, as long as they are getting sex, everything is fine and there is no reason to "rock the boat." But what about your emotional security? In order to find out where your mate's head is and where your relationship is going, it's time now to use "sex" as a weapon. Normally, I would never advise this, but this time, it's in everyone's best interest. To continue engaging in sex when there is no "clear" direction is disastrous.

Sex is a way of avoiding the problem or overlooking the problem, but in order for any loving couple to make it to their 50-year wedding anniversary, it will never happen until you occasionally use sex as a weapon.

This little technique doesn't require abstinence from sex for an extended period of time. And I promise you that you won't experience any side effects like "the munchies," your eyes bulging, hair loss, or bursting.

Before you engage in this technique, prepare your mate first. This is done by reassuring them that you enjoy them sexually, but you just want to reveal and talk through your hidden feelings. So for the next two nights (or the allotted time you need) you only want to talk in an attempt to see where you both are going and to discover the secret hang-ups they have about you. Here are the words I suggest you use:

> Sweetheart, the last thing I want to do is "turn you off" or "run you off." What I'm about to say is important, so please be honest with me. The question I want to ask you is: What is the #1 thing you dislike about me? And what can I do to make you happy or happier?

You then reassure your mate that you promise not to become angry at their response. And once your mate starts to open up, please don't interrupt them because once you become defensive, your mate will "clam up" and you'll never know their true feelings until it is too late.

Now, once your mate has finished, hug and kiss them and then reconfirm to them that you appreciate their listening to you and their honesty. Reassure them that you will make a conscious effort to improve. Afterwards, follow up with the question, "What can I do to make you happy or happier?" Once you finish, ask your mate to do the same, and of course, the same rules apply to you.

Once you are convinced and emotionally secure with your mate, then you are free to again engage in sex. From this point on, you shouldn't have any problem in achieving the "ultimate orgasm" (I'll discuss the "ultimate orgasm" is Chapter II).

Use this technique occasionally, especially when you feel that there is "distance" in your relationship. You will notice that within 30 days, you and your mate will come closer, becoming a little more patient and understanding of each other. The lines of communication will become stronger and their hidden hang-ups and gripes about you or the opposite sex will soon disappear.

Here are a few other times when *sex should be used as a weapon*:

1. When there is no commitment or monogamous relationship.

2. When a relationship has existed for 6–12 months and the only things you are getting are "promises" of a commitment.

3. When you are not sexually fulfilled and your mate is not open for discussion.

4. When "romance" and "foreplay" do not precede sex.

5. When you are abused emotionally or physically.

6. When your mate wants to spend time with you only when they are sexually aroused.

7. When you have caught your mate being unfaithful.

8. When your mate has told you the relationship is over, yet they continue to want to "sleep" with you.

9. When you have caught your mate in one lie after another.

10. When they continue to have a "roaming eye."

Sex is the most precious gift any mate can give. Under normal circumstances, sex should never be used as a weapon or an item of *negotiation, manipulation, punishment, or reward. But, as we all know, there are exceptions to every rule.*

## The 25 Most Guarded Secrets Men Never Want Women to Know

Even when you think you know your man, don't be a fool. According to 100 single men around the country, here are 25 of the most guarded secrets most men will never admit:

1. He can't stand having a female boss.

2. He doesn't have or make as much money as he pretends.

3. He's intimidated by a woman with too much power.

4. He compares her lovemaking with women he's known in the past.

5. He very seldom cuts off all contact with, or "kicks to the curb," a woman who's great in bed.

6. The only woman he truly trusts is his mother.

7. He's sometimes afraid and doesn't know what to do.

8. He believes if you want to cause a lot of confusion, have a "bunch of women" involved.

9. He often can't afford the expensive car or home he has, or he can't afford to take her out to an expensive dinner.

10. He fantasizes about having sex with two or more women.

11. He will never admit that it was he who was "dumped" or "cut loose."

12. He will spend his last dime trying to impress a woman just to get her into bed.

13. He constantly worries about another man who is better looking, has a nicer build, and/or is younger, getting his "stuff."

14. He's insecure when it comes to a woman who has more or makes more money. He will often seek a "bimbo" (a woman who is only cute with no brains) just to keep the "upper hand."

15. He brags to his friends that his woman is "secretly" taking care of him—even if he has to lie!

16. A man is a sucker for tears—and an even bigger sucker when it comes to: a pretty face, pretty eyes, full lips, a big butt, big breasts, tight jeans, and long, slender legs.

17. He can "lie" with a "straight" face and practices constantly to lie. A man will sometimes pay a friend to set up "props" and alibis to make a "good lie" believable.

18. A man tries to make up for what he's "lacking" as a person with money or gifts.

19. He worries about "growing old" alone.

20. Most men truly believe that their "worth" is what they have or who they are—e.g., doctor, lawyer, athlete, etc.—rather than the type of person they are.

21. A man is envious when his woman talks about another man who has more. He hates it when his woman describes another man as being "smart" or "handsome." (Men secretly want to "bust a cap" on Denzel Washington or Fabio.)

22. When a man passes a woman, he checks her out from the face to the boobs to the booty.

23. Most men hope to find and marry a woman with the four "B's": beauty, boobs, booty, and brains.

24. Men can't tolerate being ignored and can't stand for a woman not to be impressed by him, especially when he's "flashing" and bragging about himself.

25. A man can have a good woman at home and still want to fool around.

Looking at #25, let's talk about why this is:

1. A man has to feed his ego occasionally.

2. He has to recapture his ego.

3. He needs excitement.

4. He wants to see whether or not he still has "it."

5. Occasionally a man wants to compete with the "young boys."

6. He just wants to escape the dullness of everyday living.

7. He envies other men who are doing it and getting away with it.

8. He wants to add some "spice" to his life.

9. He wants to see whether or not he still has the "zippity-do-dah" in bed.

But don't worry—this is true only of a few men.

## Can a Man Kick a Woman to the Curb Who's Great in Bed?

Now before I answer this million-dollar question, let me first clarify what "kicking to the curb" means. It means that once you realize that you and your mate are not compatible, you walk away, leaving her alone and, more importantly, *leaving her stuff alone*!

In order to get my statistics, I had to include men from all creeds, colors, races, and socio-economic backgrounds. As a matter of fact, in the three years it took me to write this book, altogether I interviewed about 2,000 men.

When I hit them "point blank" with this question, 70% replied, "No way, Brittian. I tried, but I just can't do it. Call me 'soft,' or punk, weak, whipped, but you know, dating and relationships in the '90s has turned into either a money thing or a 'coochie' thing." And, like Tina Turner, they say, "What's love got to do with it?"

Here are the most popular reasons given by men across the country who say that they can't walk away from great sex:

1. They don't want any other man to get their good "stuff," especially their friends.

2. They don't want to start all over again, especially if he's invested a lot of time and money wining and dining her. The last thing a man wants is another man to catch his ex-woman on the rebound and get a "freebie."

3. You can find *good* sex anywhere, but *great* sex is in a class of its own.

4. A man gets emotionally attached to a woman's body.

5. A man wants a woman on the street but a "freak" in the bedroom.

After doing this survey, even I was convinced that there is some truth to the old saying, "A man's brain is between his legs." According to men across America, they can catch these women in a lie, catch her being unfaithful, catch her doing drugs, or even constantly fighting and arguing with her . . . but 70% of these same men agreed that *when it comes to great sex, they can learn to forgive and forget!*

Sexual compatibility is important in maintaining a good, healthy relationship; but as I mentioned earlier, a relationship is 90% emotional and 10% physical. When individuals see that they are not emotionally compatible and do not want the same things, it is best to break all ties, regardless of how good the "lovemaking" is. *You can find good and great sex in another relationship.* Good or great sex is an "individual call." It's what you like, or what the other person likes. To get your sex life where it is truly an "adventure" and not just another job requires honesty, commitment, and communication.

## Do Men Really Trust Women?

In a survey done with 2,000 men across America, 60% said "No!" And why?

1. Look at Adam and Eve—Eve had everything and she still wasn't satisfied.

2. Women are "weak-minded."

3. Women of the '90s will be sold to the "highest bidder."

4. Let your "stuff" get ragged, or the money get low, and your woman will be gone!

5. A woman's mother teaches them that it's all about "them" and no one else.

6. How can you trust anyone whose hormone level influences their actions and behavior?

7. Too many of their friends have helped a woman get on her feet. Once they start to do better, they turn on them and say they don't need them anymore.

8. Society and men have gotten women "spoiled rotten."

9. They want something for nothing. The "ex" gets half in a divorce. "I had money when she met me. If I had been 'broke' when we met, she wouldn't have given me the time of day!"

10. Ninety-eight percent of men surveyed—both single and married—agree that the only woman they really trust completely is their mother!

You know, it's astounding to hear there is such a large number of successful men who have such a cynical view of women of the '90s. What has happened is that too many good men have fallen victim to bad women. A woman, of course, can be responsible only for her own actions and no one else's. To reprogram your man into becoming a trusting and loving being, reinforce to him that all women are not alike. Be considerate and appreciative of him. And before you know it, he'll come around!

## Can Your Love Withstand the Rain, the Hurricane, Tornado, and Blizzard?

"Baby, you better sit down. I have some really bad news to tell you."

"Bad news? What is it, Reginald? I know whatever it is, Honey, it can't be that bad! Plus, we've made it through 'tough times' before."

"Carolyn, this time it is entirely different. The bad news is, I bought some stocks, and I really thought this stock would be a 'sure thing.' I was so confident that we would triple our investment that I invested our life savings, Keisha's college fund, and all the money I could borrow from our family and friends."

"Reginald, what are you trying to tell me?"

"Carolyn, what I'm trying to tell you is that we are *flat broke*. The stocks hit rock bottom. The ship that I thought would come in has sunk. To pay the money to the brokerage firm, we will have to sell the house, the cars, cash in all the CD's, sell your jewelry, and declare bankruptcy."

"What, Reginald? We're broke?! Bankrupt?! Wiped out?! All our money is gone? You risked everything we've worked the past 15 years for on your lame, get-rich-quick investment? Why didn't you tell me before you did it? How could you do such a foolish thing?"

"Carolyn, calm down. I feel bad enough as it is. What happened to 'Baby, we can make it through this?'"

"That person is now in the street with 'designer sheets,' sleeping under a bridge."

"Calm down, Baby, calm down. You know I've made money in the past. We started with nothing 15 years ago. Look how far we've come."

"That was *then*—this is *now*! You are 15 years older. I don't know why I married you. Oh, I remember now. You were 'funny,' sweet, and talked a lot of 'jive.' But now there's nothing 'sweet and funny' about the poor house, and you know what is worse than a 'jive-talking' man?"

"No, Baby, what is it?"

"*A jive-talking man with no money!* Mama said you were a 'Mr. Know-It-All.' She always told me one day you would bring me nothing but grief. Even Daddy tried to warn me about men like you. He said, 'Carolyn, if you hang around with nine broke people, you will surely be the tenth one.'"

"Baby, calm down. There is no need for you to rub it in. I'm sorry, Carolyn. Please calm down. It's not that bad. I've made money in the past."

"In the past 'my ass.' Even a blind squirrel gets lucky and finds one nut!"

"Baby, it's going to work out. We are a team. If we stick together, we can make it through this. We are the San Francisco 49ers, the Chicago Bulls!"

"Well, Reginald, I guess I am Deion Sanders. I'll be sold to the 'highest bidder.' I'm holding out for more money, and *I can't even say this is my house because your dumb butt just lost it!* Reginald, what were you thinking? You're a fake Mike Milliken!" (Mike Milliken was a stock broker who made millions by playing it risky.)

"All you had to do, Reginald, was 'lay the ball up,' and we could have 'chilled' until retirement. But no-o-o! Mr. Superstar wanted to be like Mike and go for a three-pointer at the buzzer, and instead of hitting nothing but the net, you threw up a brick! Well, Reginald, my darling, I'll calm down. The damage is done. There is no reason to get hysterical. I'll tell you what, 'Puddin' Face,' this is just a bad dream. I'm Dorothy in 'The Wizard of Oz,' you are the Scarecrow, the Lion, and the Tin Man. You have no brain, no courage, and no heart. And just like Dorothy, I am out of here and on my way back home to Kansas. Good-bye!"

This is an example of a woman failing to "stand by her man." We all want financial security, and any successful businessman or entrepreneur can tell you horror stories of people falling on their faces or losing the shirts off their backs.

You know, it's nice to be part of a success story. But it's great if you can make a story a success. You should at least stick around and see how the story is going to end. *It is certainly true that once you make money and lose it, you can always get it again!* So, the moral to this story is, "When the waves get high and the bills are due and everything seems hopeless, don't be a 'rat' and jump off the ship. Be an inspiration—a motivator—to your mate and help keep their sinking ship afloat. Just when you're about to throw in the towel and call it quits, that's usually the time when the storm passes."

## Why the Bad Girls Are Getting All the Good Men

Here are some of the reasons men secretly admitted as to why they wanted a bad girl:

1. Men like excitement and adventure. Less inhibited women give them that. A "free spirit" is something in all of us, but very few of us dare to "live it."

2. A man loves attention and loves to be pampered. Many women with fewer impressive credentials have the time and freedom to "stroke" their man. Professional women usually are too tired or too busy.

3. The bad girls appreciate being with you and the little things you do. Professional women tend to overlook simple things because, as we all know, "they can do for themselves."

4. Bad girls allow a man to relax and be himself. We all put on airs, but it's nice to have someone with whom you can "let your hair down."

5. They listen to a man. Men like a woman who listens to them.

6. They allow a man to take charge. Men like to feel they are in charge when sometimes they are not. It doesn't matter, as long as both people are happy.

7. They don't care about "keeping up with the Joneses" or what others may think. They don't need fancy cars, mink coats, big homes. It's just the two of you that matters.

8. Bad girls make you feel important and secure. People like to feel important, and that someone genuinely cares about them.

9. They bring out the "rebel" in you. We all have a lawless side. And it's good to let it out occasionally.

10. In lovemaking, no boundaries are set. A man wants to experience his hidden fantasies.

You know, when you're single in the '90s, you always have to be on your toes. Just because it glitters doesn't necessarily mean that it's gold. When you give too much too soon, sometimes you are "digging your own grave" or "fattening up a frog for a snake."

## Fattening up a Frog for a Snake

Your mate is unemployed, in school, between jobs, or getting ready to start his or her own business. Now, all the household and financial responsibilities rest on your shoulders. You clothe him, feed him, buy the groceries, provide shelter, transportation, pay all the bills, and fill the shoes of "mother," lover, and motivator. Why do you do it? Not because you have to, but because you love him and hope one day your investment in his future will benefit both of you. Shortly afterwards, you notice during your mate's leisure time that, instead of spending it with you or looking for a part-time job, he spends it at the beauty parlor, shopping, or "hanging out" with the fellows or just cruising around in your car. After months of this arrangement, that "anticipated" moment finally arrives. Your mate gets a job, graduates from school, or his new business begins to boom. Instead of thanking you for helping to make it all possible, he goes the other way and find someone else! Disappointed and angry, you quickly realize that all along, the only thing you were doing was "fattening up a frog for a snake." The next time, before you let anyone into your "pad," recognize the telltale signs from the start:

1. You're always "footing" the bill whenever you are together.

2. Your mate is constantly borrowing money from you and never paying it back.

3. He never wants to commit to a monogamous relationship.

4. Although you are monogamous where intimacy is concerned, the other acknowledges you as just a friend when you are out among others.

5. Your mate has an unstable residence.

6. He is overly persistent in wanting to move into your residence.

7. Your mate is always commenting on how good looking he is, and who's checking him out.

8. You buy little "thinking of you" gifts when you're out. Your mate never reciprocates.

9. Your mate has no physical transportation and is always wanting to borrow yours.

10. He is constantly telling you: "What's mine is yours and what's yours is mine"—but your part of his "mine" equals zero!

*Adrienne*

## Tips for All the Good Girls
## Who Always Seem to Pick Bad Men!

So, you think you've found your soul mate, that "Mr. Right" has finally "popped" the big question! He is the perfect man, he is handsome, kind, sensitive, wants a family and, to put the icing on the cake, he has a job! No more single life for you! It is now a husband, kids, a house, a dog, and "living happily ever after." Sounds like your dream come true? Now, before you rush off and pick your bridesmaids, let's back up a little and make sure first of all that you picked the "right" man. As you know, 50% of all marriages end in divorce. Every day you hear about that "Prince Charming" who rode into someone's life on a white horse, and who turns out to be a "frog," later being forced to leave handcuffed in the back of a police car. If you are a good girl who always seems to pick a bad man, before you say "I do," make sure he *doesn't* do any of the following:

1. Can't hold a steady job, is always between jobs, or is always "getting ready" to start his own business. For a relationship to last, each person must do his or her fair share.

2. Insecure or excessively jealous. We are all a little insecure and a little jealous of someone else wanting our mate. It is healthy and "keeps us on our toes." But if you can't have male friends, or if you keep getting the "third degree" whenever another man looks at you, you'd better put your wedding plans on hold.

3. Make sure you are on the same educational level, or at least want the same things out of life. Statistics have shown that there are more educated females than males, so often your "Mr. Right" may not have a college degree. Intelligence is not always measured in degrees. Most millionaires did not

make their money with degrees, but with hard work. Just make sure your man is secure with your educational level and with himself, and everything should be fine.

4. Uses drugs or drinks excessively. You already know the answer to that one. We don't even have to go into it.

5. Has a good job but is always broke. Let's face it. The biggest fight newlyweds have is usually over money. Make sure you check out your man's spending and saving habits.

6. Has a bad temper he can't control. If a man can't control his temper while he is single, what will happen with the added pressures of a wife, kids, and a house?

7. Constantly comparing you to old girlfriends. Is he marrying you or marrying on the rebound because he can't have her?

8. He has no spiritual belief in God or a higher being. Sometimes life is going to throw you a curve, and the only thing that is going to get you through those trying times is faith. Spiritual belief will always get you through. "Tough times don't last, but tough people do."

9. Make sure he's not in trouble with the law. Let's face facts. "Boys will be boys," and often men will have had an infraction with the law; but that is no real big problem. I just don't want you to end up with Ted Bundy's brother or someone who needs to hide out for a few years.

10. Make sure your "sweet baby" is also your buddy or friend; there's nothing more beautiful than to be able to communicate with someone else, tell your problems to, and act crazy with.

If your man passes the "pop quiz" with at least a "C," then it's all good, and you'd better choose your bridesmaids. If he got a "D" or worse, don't be fooled. Just because it looks good and shines like a diamond, it could one day turn out to be a diamel or fake. Before you say "I do," take this "pop quiz" to make sure he *doesn't* do!

Being in a relationship or being in love can cause anyone to scream or pull their hair out!

## Tips for Being *in Love* with a Mate That *You Can't Stand!*

Have you ever had a mate that you were in love with or were physically or sexually attracted to, and everyone thought that you made the perfect couple . . . but their "attitude," selfishness, and "over-inflated ego" was a real turn-off? Or have you had a mate that you've been involved with for awhile who doesn't respect you, or treats you like dirt, keeping you on an "emotional rollercoaster?" You want to leave, but you can't, and every day with them is a game of "guess my mood." Sounds familiar? Sounds like your relationship? Before you dial 9-1-1, don't feel like the "Lone Ranger." Thousands of people are suffering with the same problem. This problem is best diagnosed as *"Being in love with a mate that you can't stand."*

If you have this problem, the best treatment is to catch it in its infancy. Some early symptoms of this illness can be recognized by your mate's constantly using the pronouns "I" or "me" instead of "us" or "we." Perhaps your man is "prettier" than you. Perhaps your mate is always looking around to see who is admiring him or "checking him out." Or maybe your mate has forgotten special occasions such as birthdays, anniversaries, or is constantly making—then breaking—promises.

If this situation has gone from infancy to adulthood—and is now "malignant" or "terminal," let me call the "specialist."

Relationships are about being happy for both people involved. The person you have now may look great on your arm and turn heads when you are out, or make you call 9-1-1 in bed. But just as they cause your rocket to ignite, he can also cause your rocket to crash. Remember that love is 90% emotional and 10% physical. It's two people sharing, giving of themselves unselfishly. It's not one person always giving and the other person always receiving. Even though you may love them, you need to love yourself first. You know what it takes to make you happy, and at this point in your life, you should be looking for commitment, stability, and emotional and financial security. You don't have the time to "babysit" or psychoanalyze someone. So before you sink to the bottom emotionally, abandon ship and swim to safety and let the "captain" go down with the ship.

When it comes to love, very few people can find a "perfect 10." Sometimes you have to settle for a "7" and work with the rest.

For Women Only

## You Can Dress Him up but You Can't Take Him to the White House

How often have you said, "My man would be perfect if he didn't . . ." or "John makes me so angry because he doesn't . . ." or "When John does . . . it gets on my 'last nerve.'"

You know, we can all stand some improvement. We all have some little idiosyncrasies that drive our mates crazy. If this describes your man—"You can dress him up, but you can't take him to the White House"—here are a few hints on etiquette that will bring you and your man from last on the "social ladder" all the way up to #1. Then, if you don't get an invitation from the President, you'll know it's not because of him!

1. His knowledge of food is limited, and his table manners are horrible. He doesn't know "sushi" from salmon. This is definitely a "no-no." It's almost as bad as saying, "Will you please pass the jelly?" To improve his knowledge of food and fine dining awareness, you should start off first by "dining fine." Encourage him to take you out to dinner. Encourage him to experiment with different entrees or exotic foods. And ladies, make sure that he doesn't order a hamburger. At home, practice setting a formal meal and teach him positioning of forks and spoons, and which one to use for what dish.

2. You can't stand the way he dresses! If there's one candidate for the "fashion police," it's your man. The '60s were great, but now they're gone, and your man has left the farm years ago. To get him to change to a "modern" look, first compliment him on things that you like about him. Then casually mention that you think he would look great in . . . and then take him shopping and buy it for him. Remember, it's not what you say, but how you say it, that gets results.

3. He "swears" a lot and uses incorrect English. When one of those four-letter words comes out, or he splits an infinitive, correct him. Often people develop habits and are unaware of them. Constantly bring this to his attention.

4. He can't dance, and instead of being Fred Astaire or Michael Jackson, he is simply "Fred"—everyone is staring at you. Please "moonwalk" us off the dance floor and let's "beat it."

5. He is not informed on current events. To get your man informed on something other than a Chicago Bulls statistic, have dinner in front of the TV during news and discuss current events while you're eating.

6. He drinks excessively and gets "loud" and obnoxious. Nothing will get you kicked out of the White House faster than a loud, drunken man offending all the guests. Put your man on a 1- or 2-drink maximum restriction, and keep your eye on him just to make sure he adheres to it.

So, if you have a man whom you can dress up and dare to take to the White House, here you have a few etiquette hints to follow. If you still don't receive an invitation from the White House, at least you can feel confident that it's not because of your man!

## How to Have a "Happy Meal" When You Bring Home More Bacon and Your Husband—A Few Beans

You're now at the top of your career. You're a manager, executive, CEO, or Vice President. Your financial dream is now a reality. You got that promotion, you're getting paid, and you're proud. But at home, you have problems, and you're puzzled. Why? It's your husband. His salary is considerably less than yours. You bring home more bacon, and he brings home only a few beans; and around the dinner table, it's never a "happy meal."

Just the mention of the word "money" causes him to get hysterical or depressed. He is constantly insecure about your paying the bulk of the household expenses. It has even affected your intimate moments together. How do you juggle the "boardroom" and the "bedroom?"

The problem is not your getting paid. The problem is that he is insecure and disappointed with himself. A man who truly loves his woman wants her to "achieve the moon" because, if this makes her happy, then she can make him happy. In order to make someone else happy, you must first be happy with yourself, your man needs to develop his fullest potential much like you had to develop yours.

We all have "shortcomings" that prevent us from fulfilling our dreams or financial goals. It may be education, poor communication skills, or not being able to get along well with others. Someone else can see the things that we can't see in ourselves. If this is the problem that's keeping your man from advancing:

1. Talk to him about pursuing an advanced degree, more job or trade skills, or even help him open his own business. Remember, it's all going in the same pot, regardless of who brings it home.

2. Always reinforce to him the positive things you like about him.

3. Always seek his advice when you are making decisions, regardless of how trivial.

4. Be supportive of him and the contributions he makes to the household, but never ever go for the jugular by throwing your salary up in his face. Once you do that, it won't matter how much bacon or beans you both bring home—you'll never have a "happy meal."

In relationships, it's vital to keep an open mind and be flexible. Following is an example of a problem that I once had to solve.

## Choosing Between My Two Favorite Girls—
## My Mate and My Mother—
## Whom Would You Choose?

My mother couldn't stand my mate! My mate said my mother was always putting her nose in our business. My mother told me my girl is out for what she can get and would bring me nothing but grief! My mate said my mother is overstepping her boundaries, and I should stop being a "mama's boy" and be a man! What should I do? Should you choose the woman who gave you life and who you know will be with you through "thick and thin?" Or should you choose the girl whom you dearly love and can't imagine living life without?

I called a few disc jockeys around the United States and asked them to survey 100 single men in eight cities: New York, Miami, Cleveland, Atlanta, Chicago, Detroit, Los Angeles, and New Orleans. Here are the results of the survey:

1. In New York, 65% of the single men said it's "mom all the way." Thirty-five percent would choose their mates.

2. In Miami, a whopping 80% chose their dear old mother.

3. In Cleveland, 70% of the single men gave mom two thumbs up, and only 30% chose their mate.

4. In "Hotlanta," Georgia, 50% chose mom while the other 50% chose their mate.

5. In Chicago, 80% of the single men said "mom is still the favorite girl."

6. In Detroit, mom had to take a back seat to the mate in 60% of the cases.

7. In Los Angeles, it was a 50-50 "slug-out" between mom and the mate.

8. In New Orleans, it's "Mother's Day" all day long! Seventy percent of the single men said their mates would have to eat "gumbo" when it comes to their mothers.

Men have always been attached to their mothers. Even as children, we played a game called the "dozens" in which children talk about each other's parents. You could talk about "daddy" all day, but don't even go there with "mom." What is this thing men have with their mothers?

Today, a lot of homes are headed by single parents, usually the mother. The mother is not only a little boy's provider, but she is his motivator, inspiration, and his biggest dream is to grow up one day and make mom proud of him. Do you notice when superstars get an award, "mom" is up there next to "God?" That's a pretty high position for anyone to be placed in! And yet, through "thick and thin," mom will always be there when everyone else leaves or turns their back on you. Just like a woman, men want emotional and unconditional love, and if you can find a mate who loves you "half" as much as your mother, then you've found the "perfect" woman.

To get next to a man who is a bonafide, 100% "mama's boy," a woman must have a little patience. The problem with this man is that he distrusts people, especially women. He's either been severely hurt, or has constantly heard horror stories about women.

To keep your man from running to his mother every five minutes, and to keep his mother out of your business, you will have to tell your man how much you love him, care about him, and genuinely want to make him happy. Even better than that, show him! Don't put him in a position of having to choose between the two. You are a family, and marriage is a combination of families. If he truly loves you, he will give his mother the respect, but he will eventually come around and give you the love. In my own experience, I had to learn this and do it.

## The Ten Cities Where 65% of Married Spouses Cheat the Most

Are you truly faithful to your spouse? This is one of those things that makes you want to say, "Hmmmm!" All of us want to feel secure about our relationship. Thus, we cringe at the thought of our mates being unfaithful. Let's be honest with ourselves. We all fantasize about our favorite singer or movie star, or we go to a bar or club and enjoy flirting and "window shopping." But this is all harmless. Well, maybe not! I don't know about that!

In a recent survey conducted in ten major cities across the country:

1. Atlanta
2. Washington, D.C.
3. Los Angeles
4. Detroit
5. Chicago
6. Dallas
7. Cleveland
8. St. Louis
9. Philadelphia
10. Las Vegas

Sixty-five percent of the men and women interviewed admitted that they have had, or were involved in an extra-marital affair. Sound shocking? Well, what's even more astounding are the reasons given. Here are ten of the most frequent responses. For women, the reasons were:

1. I can't communicate with my husband.

2. My spouse does not notice me, spend enough quality time with me, or no longer makes me feel attractive or sexy.

3. Marriage boredom: He works, he comes home, he eats, he watches TV, and he sleeps. Tomorrow, it's the same routine over and over again.

4. Sexual boredom: no creativity or adventure.

5. Infrequent lovemaking. He's very seldom in the mood.

For men, the reasons were:

1. My wife is very unappreciative.

2. My spouse doesn't show me enough affection or pay me enough attention.

3. She's self-centered and selfish in bed, or a "prima donna."

4. I want to see whether I still "have it."

5. I'm a "dog"—I need more than one woman to be happy!

To keep a spouse faithful in the '90s requires a little work—you must invest as much time in your relationship as you spend in advancing your career. Love is like a flower: it must be fertilized and tended to on a daily basis if it is going to grow. If that love is ignored or abused, it will die, and the only thing left are memories of what was.

A couple should spend quality time together, noticing each other, and try to reenact how they were when they first met. Remember, the thing it took to get your baby hooked in the first place is the same thing it will take to keep her. (I will explore other ways to keep your spouse faithful in the section, "How to Get and Keep Your Man at Home, Trained, Whipped, Faithful, and on a Leash.")

## How to Tell If Your Mate Is "Cheating" or an Out-of-Control Dog

In the '90s, you must be able to recognize from the start that if your "harmless little Chihuahua" has some "pitbull potential." Here are some telltale signs:

1. They are constantly saying, "I need more time to myself"—especially if you only see them a few days out of the week already.

2. They're always working late, but the "time" is not reflected in their paycheck.

3. They're always finding excuses to be away from you. It's "the girls and I" or "the fellas and I are supposed to get together."

4. They are never, or very rarely, in the mood for sex, especially if you know they enjoy it.

5. They suddenly become critical of you or are comparing you to other people.

6. They try to start an argument over trivial or insignificant matters, then storm from the house angry.

7. They develop a certain interest in new things.

8. He or she has "roving" eyes.

9. You notice an unfamiliar fragrance in their hair or on their clothes.

10. They can't look you in the eye when you ask them, point-blank, "Are you having an affair?"

It is easy to keep a "potential dog" on a leash. And it is just as easy to train them from the start to "heel," "obey," and "stay at home." This method will work even with the fierce competition from other top "pedigrees" who are busy "wagging their tails" in front of your man or "whistling" at your lady.

You have to "train" your mate early in your relationship to be a woman's best friend.

Be honest from the start. Be loving, affectionate, physically in shape, sexy, pleasant, considerate, and romantic. Then, make lovemaking a "21-gun salute." I'll use a paraphrase of a slogan the U.S. Army made famous: Don't make lovemaking just another job; make lovemaking an adventure, and be all that you can be. Be there emotionally for your mate and become his best friend. The man of the '90s will occasionally "window shop" or "flirt" from time to time, but it's just clean fun. It's only to feed his ego. And it's good for his self-esteem. But when you know you deserve a "blue ribbon" at the "dog show," when the other women's "tails" are "wagging" and the other dogs are misbehaving, you can still make your little "Chihuahua" behave, come at command, sit in a corner, roll over, play dead, bark only when he's told, fetch, and stay close to home.

## Why Men "Dog" Women

Before we go into the reasons men "dog" women, let us first explain the terminology "dog." To "dog" a woman means to "knowingly misuse or abuse her whether it is emotionally or physically."

Why a man would knowingly "dog" a woman could be for one or for several reasons; but the top ten are:

1. His mother was never around to give him the love and attention he craved. As a result, he now resents *all* women and takes his frustration and anger out on all of them.

2. His father often abused his mother, and he now thinks it is the "manly" thing to do.

3. Often he saw his mother degrading herself with different men, and now he has little or no respect for women in general.

4. Sometimes a man wants to "crush" the ego of an overly attractive woman so that she becomes open to "change" and "improvement."

5. He feels a need to "get even" for that "one special woman" who "dropped" him or hurt him deeply.

6. He is trying to find out how much a woman really loves him. He feels if she takes his abuse, then she truly loves him; otherwise, if she didn't love him, she would leave rather than take the abuse.

7. Sometimes a man feels the need to keep the "upper hand." He thinks that if the woman doesn't think he cares, she will work extra hard to please him.

8. The man may have had experiences which make him want to "pay back" all the women who made him feel they were "too good" for him, or women who made him feel he would "never amount to anything," even though now the man may be successful.

9. Sometimes a man is simply trying to avoid all emotional attachments.

10. Some men feel that "dogging" is the way to play the "dating game"; you either "dog" or "get dogged."

On the other hand, no woman should have to go through or take any abuse from a man just because she is "lonely," suffering from low self-esteem, or just because her man has "hang-ups" about the opposite sex.

To tell if a man is a potential abusive mate:

1. Notice his actions at the beginning of a relationship. Remember that what is in a person's heart will eventually come out through their mouths and their actions.

2. Ask him point-blank what he thinks of women.

3. Notice how he treated the women before you (examples: his mother, his sisters, etc.).

4. Listen to the comments he makes about women.

5. Notice what he says to you and does to you when he is angry.

Remember: If you don't have any respect for yourself, nobody else will either.

## The Most Popular Places Spouses Go to Cheat

When I surveyed hundreds of cheating spouses around the country, they openly admitted there are "favorite spots" they often go to in order to cheat:

1. The Internet and E-mail. As we head into the year 2000, the Internet and E-mail will have a whole new usage.

2. Over at a relative's house. Remember, "Blood is thicker than water." Very few family members are going to "bust their kin."

3. Lunch break on the job. Since very few couples of the '90s have time to see their mates for lunch, lunch time is now becoming an ideal time to meet a lover. In fact, hundreds of couples around the country have been cheating for years and their mates haven't suspected a thing.

4. At the gym.

5. At the mall.

6. At sports events.

7. At the airport.

8. At the beauty salon.

9. At the grocery store.

10. At a bowling alley.

11. On business trips.

12. At hotels.

13. On the bus or subway.

14. At the park.

15. Going for a walk or jogging.

## Overcoming an Abusive Relationship: "I Am Somebody and Deserve to Be Loved"

At some point in time, we will all be rejected, "dumped," "dogged," or come out of a relationship with "egg on our face." When the inevitable finally happens to you, don't be too hard on yourself. Don't feel as though you are "undesirable" or undeserving to be loved.

If you have done everything you can to make someone else happy, then who's the fool? Them or you? Just because you have failed doesn't necessarily mean you are a failure. When one door closes, another one opens.

To prepare yourself for the next relationship, you must first overcome your present anger, negativity, and doubt. So, the next time you are about to take that giant step, repeat the following over and over just to "reassure" yourself that you are truly worthy of being loved:

> I am somebody and deserve to be loved. I am unique, one of a kind, and can't be compared to anyone else. What I'm offering is my devotion, friendship, and unconditional love. When I look into the mirror, I like what I see; I see a person who deserves to be loved, and that person is "me." I have a good heart, a good head on my shoulders, and I want something out of life. I know I'm not the most attractive person, but I'll make someone a good wife.
>
> It's a long journey in finding a soul mate, and I guess patience is the key. But until I find my soul mate, I refuse to be abused and misused . . . because the real 'Lotto' is to find a loving and caring person like me.

## How to Quench the Thirst for an Old Flame and Set Your Current Romance on Fire!

You know, a few years ago, I ran into an old girlfriend I'll call "Cathy." I hadn't seen Cathy in ten years. But back then, Cathy was "all of that" and a plate of potato salad on the side! Cathy had my "nose open" and "whipped." She was a nice girl with naughty girl qualities. Although I had the "hots" for Cathy, I knew Cathy wasn't "mom" material, or the type of woman I needed long-term.

Well, ten years later, someone gave Cathy my number, and I received an unexpected call from her. When Jennifer, my new girl, gave me the message, my heart jumped. As the days passed, curiosity began to get the best of me, and Jennifer, too, saw a change in my personality. Of course, Jennifer knew about Cathy because we had discussed our old flames before we became involved.

Finally, I told Jennifer that I had to resolve this matter. *This is what you should do, too, if you still have the "hots" for an old flame:*

1. *See your old flame.* Face your problem. You can't hide it, and if it is not resolved, your new relationship can't grow.

2. *Understand why you want to see them.* (a) Do you want to see if the attraction is still there? (b) Do you want an "apology" or to apologize? (c) Do you want to rub their nose in your success? (d) Do you want to "kick their butt" for hurting or leaving you? (e) If your motive is revenge, the best revenge without fail is to live well.

3. When you see them, look sharp! Maintain your composure. If your heart still flutters, you still have the "hots." Think with the brain in your head. If you're still hooked, never let them know it. If you are single at the time, you might tell them you still find them attractive;

but don't go any further than that at your initial meeting. Let them lead. Since you are involved in a relationship, tell them why you came. If you still harbor hurt and pain from the past, express it to them. Sometimes you have to move backwards in order to move forward. Usually, with growth comes maturity. Sometimes all you want from that person is an apology. Keep in mind, too, that relationships don't *not* work because the "timing is off." If both of you are single at the time and there is still "chemistry," give it a chance. But I also must warn you, "History has a way of repeating itself." If that person still hasn't matured or changed, kill the relationship. *If you are currently involved in a relationship* and you talk of "old times," and there are pleasant memories and the "chemistry" is still there, *don't even think about jeopardizing what you have.* Whatever you do, do not take a "roll in the hay" or jump their bones for "old time's sake." If you read and follow my instructions in this chapter, you will have no reason to move backwards. That was then, this is now. Continue to move forward. Put them and your old relationship in the past, or in the category of "education"—or, in most cases, in the class of "stupidity." Remember, love is sometimes a misunderstanding between two fools!

4. Be honest with your current mate. Allow them to fill that void. Give your current mate the opportunity to arouse that flame, that passion, or the "bad girl" that your old flame used to bring out within you.

5. Thank your new love morning, noon, and night for being the kind of person who could be secure, strong, and supportive enough to allow you to resolve this problem.

Also, thank God and consider yourself blessed because you have truly found your soul mate. That is what I, too, had to do. "Cathy" is "gone with the wind," and now, frankly, I don't give a damn!

## How to Get a 50-Year Warranty with Your Marriage and a Maintenance Plan Free of Break up or Break down

Wouldn't it be nice if marriage was like a new Mercedes—carrying a lifetime warranty? Or like a BMW—you had a "warning light" or "breaking system" to notify you of oncoming danger. Wouldn't it be nice if marriage was like a new Lexus, Cadillac, or Lincoln? Always dependable, always giving you a "smooth ride," and you didn't have to worry about any bumps? Wouldn't it be great if marriage had a "Government Protection Plan" so that if you were not totally satisfied with your spouse, you could have them "recalled." Despite the curves, the mountains, and valleys, marriage is still the most popular highway traveled. Now many "enthusiastic motorists" have traveled down the road of matrimony. But for whatever reason, before they hit "50," they've had a "blow up" or "blow out." Well, I've talked to some of those "happy motorists" for whom marriage has lasted 50 years, and according to them, this is how they got a warranty with their marriages:

1. They did their daily maintenance. For example, "Baby, I love you. Here's a big hug. That means last night was really 'kicking.' Tonight, I'm taking you out to dinner. Tomorrow night, I'm washing the dishes."

2. You must abide by God's law. If you don't, God will not honor your lifetime warranty, and your policy (your marriage) will soon be cancelled (divorce).

3. Show your mate as much attention as the children. Remember, the only difference between a man and a boy is the cost and size of the toys. Make sure you pacify your spouse as well.

4. Never have any secret bank accounts or residences.

5. Never belittle your mate when your friends are around.

6. Let your children see you share in the household responsibilities.

7. To ensure that your marriage makes it to that 50-year mark, and keep your warranty active, you must frequently go in for a "tune up." Make sure the doctor checks your values (heart) to ensure that it's ticking properly. Then check your oil (blood) to make sure you're not a quart high (high blood pressure) or a quart low (need iron). Also, during your annual "tune up," make sure you haven't picked up a foreign substance in your gas tank, such as sugar.

8. Include your spouse in your work and always ask his opinion. Even if he is not an expert, he will appreciate you for valuing his opinion.

9. Make child-rearing a responsibility for both of you.

10. Back him up when he puts his foot down with the kids. No means no. Kids are slick when it comes to playing parents against each other. "Daddy said no, but we know Mommy is a sucker for a 'sob story' and a cute smile."

11. Help your spouse achieve their "separate" dream. Don't take the attitude that "I've made it; therefore, we are happy."

12. If you enter into marriage with the attitude of what someone can do for you, then this is a "manufacturer's defect," and it's not covered by your warranty. Also, your

spouse will soon grow tired of you, regardless of how good you look. He will soon want to take you back to the "dealer," your mother, or from whomever he got you.

13. There's no mate like a spouse who makes a lot of unnecessary noise such are arguing, keeping up "stuff," or staying angry and will not tell you why. If you have a problem, discuss it. If you don't want to discuss it, let silence fill the air and just let your engine purr. Everyone loves a little peace and quiet.

14. If you are a CEO or executive, the boardroom stops at home. At home, you share the power. The king and queen rule together. There is no dictatorship or anything else.

15. Put God first and your family second.

16. Trust and honesty are a must! Often you will be apart. You should wonder only "**how**" your mate is doing, not "**what**" your mate is doing.

17. Try to grow together and not apart. This can be accomplished by your becoming interested in his hobbies and including him in your "girl talk."

18. Reinforce to your mate that you still find him desirable and very attractive. This will cause him to work extra hard to stay that way.

19. When your mate is in a foul mood, balance it off with a positive attitude and a big hug. Remember, it takes two to argue.

20. Make your children part of your life and not your entire life. Remember, one day, they will leave home.

21. Don't panic on the "highway of matrimony" when debris, bumps, hills and other obstacles get in your way. This is the time you should buckle up, pull together, and rely on your "air bag" . . . faith.

22. Don't be fooled by those young "hot rods" (young women). They require high maintenance and are not very dependable. Remember, as time progresses, your spouse will go up in value, and everyone wants to have a "classic" one day.

23. Pick one day out of each month and make that "his" special day for the rest of his life. (On that particular day, his wish is your command.)

24. Take him shopping and keep his wardrobe in style.

25. Never let anyone—neither family nor friends—belittle your spouse in your presence.

26. Make your mate feel like everyday is his birthday, Christmas, or Valentine's Day. If he loves sports, buy two tickets to a game.

27. Call your mate at work and ask him or her for a date.

28. Find out something your mate has always wanted and, if it's affordable, buy it for them.

29. Always reinforce the positive things you like about your mate and help him or her work on the negative things.

30. When your mate is busy, or you feel that you are being neglected, put on something sexy, drag him off to the bedroom, and "rock his world."

31. Anticipate his needs. For example, "Sweetheart, did you take your medicine today? Please do it for me. Remember when we got married, we promised to be married for 50 years and live to be 100." Or, "Baby, you have been working so hard. I tell you what—why don't you go out with the fellows and I'll keep the kids. Don't worry—here's a little money. Go ahead and 'paint the town.' Come to think of it, since we're on a budget, you'd better use 'cheap paint!' Or, if you can get a can of spray paint ... well, spray paint costs money, too. Honey, get a box of crayons and instead of painting the town, just write graffiti on the wall. Just kidding, Baby. That was a joke. It made you laugh, so it was worth the effort. Go out tonight and have a good time."

32. Come home early, unexpectedly, and grab—or kidnap!—your spouse and take them to a romantic hideaway or to a hotel and have a scandalous affair with him or her.

33. Always be honest with your mate—the truth will set you free, not set you up, remember?

34. The words "I love you" will never grow old.

35. Every year, renew your wedding vows to each other in an intimate ceremony over a romantic dinner. For example, "I will always love, honor, and cherish you until death do us part, or our 50-year warranty expires, whichever comes first."

So, happy 50th anniversary! And keep these helpful hints in mind. Your 50-year warranty will always be in effect, your marriage will never "blow up" or "break down," your spouse will remain devoted, faithful, and after 50 years of marriage, your mate will be a "classic," in a class of his own, and you'll never have to worry about your mate trading you in for one of those young "hot rods."

## How to Keep Your Man at Home, Trained, Whipped, Faithful, and on a Leash

You come home from work tired, exhausted, and cranky. Your mouth suddenly drops open and you wonder whether you are in the right house. You see, the house you left earlier that morning was in mayhem. The home you are in now can easily qualify for *Better Homes and Garden* magazine. The dishes are washed, the beds are made, and the smell of potpourri lingers in the air. Dinner is on the table. As your man hands you a glass of "bubbly," you drink and laugh as the bubbles tickle your nose. He then picks you up and, before you know, your legs are wrapped around his waist and you are now riding him like the Lone Ranger on Silver! You whisper to him so the kids in the other room won't hear you. As he pinches your butt, he turns suddenly from a "nice man" into an "animal," an "octopus," and you love it. Kisses shower your body, and you think to yourself, "If your man had committed a crime and the FBI was looking for him, they could get his fingerprints from any part of your body." He then whispers in your ear, "Baby, I have been thinking about you all day long. Once we get upstairs, there will be a lot of heavy breathing and a lot of screaming. So, Sharon, you better be gentle with me while I'm 'screaming.'"

As you both laugh, you tell him, "If you're afraid, you need to get a dog! If you can't run with the big dogs, you better stay on the porch and just bark! Ruff! Ruff!" You continue, telling him, "This is a Wendy's hamburger, and I have something hot and juicy for you. Or I'll pretend it's Burger King so you can 'have it your way.' And Bobby, before it's all over, we both will know how many 'licks' it takes to get to the center of a 'Tootsie Roll Pop'—let's see . . . one, two . . . you are so-o-o bad!" Then, as he sweeps you into his arms and takes you passionately upstairs, you feel like Scarlett O'Hara in "Gone With The Wind." Immediately you begin to act out your own little role: "Bobby, you rascal, put me down! You can't come home from work and 'ravage' my body. I won't stand for it! You hear me?"

Twitching his mouth like Clark Gable, he says with a southern drawl, "Sharon, you can call a SWAT team, the Los Angeles Police Department, or anyone you like, and I still won't give a damn!"

"Oh, Bobby, you are such a rascal!"

Arriving at the top of the stairs, you see candlelight lining the hallway along with rose petals like the bread crumbs in the story of "Hansel and Gretel." As he takes you to the bedroom, you hear Luther Vandross singing on the stereo. The song "Let Me Hold You Tight" fills the room, and you whisper in his ear, "Luther, Luther. . . ." At the mere mention of another man's name, your husband becomes insanely jealous, and before you know it, he's now competing with Luther Vandross for your affection. You laugh and giggle as your man begins to sing "Let me hold you tight, if only for one night . . ." and continues to serenade you off-key. Finally, you make it to the bedroom where you see red satin sheets, more candles, and another glass of "bubbly." Your husband lays you gently on the bed and kisses you gently, then gives you a sip of the champagne. As he begins to sing loudly, "I won't tell a soul, no one has to know, it will be all right, if only for one night. . . ." He's taking off your blouse, pretending to spill the champagne on your chest. The "bubbly" starts its "seductive" journey down the canals of your body. Your body begins to quiver. Then, on cue, "Bobby Vandross" sets your body aflame, his tongue exploring everywhere, and now he's in the "captain's chair" and attempting bodily to go where no man has gone before. Looking over your body, he smiles, and his tongue continues to explore "strange life forms." He massages your aching feet, caresses your big toe, tickles your little toe, then whispers, "Baby, you are so beautiful, and you look good enough to eat!" His tongue moves up your leg, and he begins his journey to forbidden space when, suddenly, you hear "Buzz! Buzz!" It's your alarm clock.

It's 6:00 in the morning. It's time for work. Darn! It was only a dream! As you adjust to reality, you gaze at your "real life" husband lying next to you, dressed in hole-riddled boxer shorts, snoring with his mouth open. You think to yourself, "How do I get my real-life husband to be like that 'passionate' man in my dream? And how do I keep him at home, trained, whipped, faithful, and on a leash?"

1. All the "special" attention you enjoy—do the same for him. Men and women both enjoy the same things. For example, greet him at the door with a big smile. "How was your day?" Then give him a hot wet one right on the "kisser." Pretend that you are his personal "genie" and grant him three wishes.

2. Keep your personal appearance up. Exercise, keep that body in tip-top shape—"work-it-baby" shape. If your man is in love with you and still in "lust" with your body, wear clothes around the house or out (that's if he's secure with your relationship). This gives him a "peep show" and reveals the "curves," the hips, breasts, or legs. Be sexy!

3. Turn him on even more with your mind. Be able to handle business. Men love to brag to their friends how their woman has it "going on." Additionally, it gives a man a sense of security to know if he slips, you can take up the slack.

4. Call him at the office unexpectedly, just to "flirt" with him or "talk dirty." Example: "Sweetheart, I know you're busy, but did I accidentally leave my panties in your briefcase? Oops! Silly me! Now I have to walk around all day with nothing on! I guess I'll just sit here naked until you bring them to me. By the way, I'm standing in front of the window, talking to you on the cordless. I just can't seem to get these old drapes to close. I sure hope the neighbors don't see. Bye now!"

5. Always say "please" when you ask him to do something for you. The word "please," said in a sweet voice, can get a man to do almost anything. For example, "Baby, will

you buy me a Rolls Royce Corniche—please, Baby? Let me spend your entire paycheck shopping—please? Baby, can I throw your inconsiderate mother out in the cold? Pretty please?!" He responds, "Okay, Baby, throw the old bag of bones out!"

To keep a man faithful is simple:

1. Use guilt: "Baby, if I found out you were unfaithful to me, I don't think I could ever get over it. In fact, 'Punkin,' you are the only man that I have ever trusted in my life."

2. *Let his own insecurities keep him in check.* "You know your friend, Jerry? I can tell that he likes me. But since you are faithful to me, I would never think of looking at another man. Now that we have that clear, tell your friend Jerry to stop wearing his jeans so tight!"

3. Constantly tell your man, "Baby, you can always depend on, trust, and believe in me. All I ask is for you to be honest and be true, and you'll never have to worry about me going anywhere or doing anything!"

Now when it comes to getting a man "whipped" or getting him where he neither desires nor thinks of another woman, this, too, is simple.

While your man is relaxed, ask him to reveal his wildest sexual fantasy. If he's shy, keep asking him. You might want to get the ball rolling by first revealing one of your fantasies. Give it to him play-by-play, censoring nothing. If he is still shy or reluctant, get bold! "woman-handle" him! It's the '90s! Nice girls are for wimps. If he's afraid, then he'd better get a dog. At this moment, do something to him that you've never done before. Forget the "good girl" stuff your mother told you about—take it to the extreme. At that point, his brain will record that moment forever. Finally, put the icing on the cake by saying something that will send subliminal messages to him, like: "Sweetheart, you know that little 'treat?' . . . Well, it is reserved only for you."

You know, it's a funny thing about a woman. When she finds out she's been lied to and cheated on, there's no telling what she would do in a moment of weakness. As you allow silence to fill the room, that little subliminal message—along with the thought of another man getting his "num-nums"—will finally register in his brain and hit him like a ton of bricks. Before you know it, you're the only "diva" in his life, his only "chick on the side," his only girlfriend, his only "other woman," his only "freak of the week," and the only girl he goes to for a "quickie."

If you follow all these examples, not only will you keep your man at home, trained, whipped, faithful, and on a leash, but your man is now "house-broken" and can easily be taught other useful tricks like cooking, cleaning, doing the laundry, changing diapers, taking out the garbage, mowing the lawn, "fetching," telling the truth, refraining from chasing women in sports cars, and not to go running and "sniffing" after every "wagging tail" that comes his way! When it comes to dating in the '90s, it's a "dog-eat-dog" world. You either think like a dog or you get dogged!

## How to Have the "Ultimate Orgasm"

In order for a relationship to truly survive or pass the "test of time," both parties must be sexually fulfilled. According to a 1995 survey done by Masters and Johnson, 62% of American women admitted they had faked an orgasm. Furthermore, a 1996 survey conducted by *Cosmopolitan* magazine revealed that sexual boredom was one of the reasons given by both men and women as to why they cheat.

Earlier I mentioned that sex is 90% emotional and 10% physical. And this 90/10 rule is also true when it comes to trying to achieve the "ultimate orgasm." The process must begin *before* you reach the bedroom.

1. For a woman, the ultimate orgasm begins with *commitment and a monogamous relationship.* In order for a woman to truly become a "diva" or an exotic fantasy, she must first be emotionally secure within the relationship.

2. *Romance!* Nothing prepares a woman for that desired moment more than her mate's making love to her "head" and "heart" first. This includes: open communication, honesty, flowers, flirting with her, buying her a new dress or an outfit that you would like to see her wear, or sweeping her up in your arms every day.

3. For a man, the ultimate orgasm begins with *appreciation*— reinforce to him the things he does that turn you on and reveal to him other "spices" that you dream about.

Now that you are both emotionally prepared, let's concentrate on the physical part. As you reveal your secret fantasies and turn-ons, close your eyes and forget about satisfying yourself. Concentrate only on satisfying your mate. If both parties do the same thing, what you now have are two people giving of themselves unselfishly. Before you know it, the two of you will truly experience the ultimate orgasm.

Keep in mind the three steps to achieving the ultimate orgasm: Commitment, romance, and appreciation. Remember: You can find "good" sex anywhere, but "great" sex is in a class of its own!

## "Getting Your Freak on!"

As you get older, you will reach a point in your life when you look back over your accomplishments and ask yourself, "Is this it? What have I done that is of any real significance? Is this all the money I am ever going to make? I have gone as far as I can go in my career. My time and my life are spent making someone else happy. Nobody cares about me. I am not appreciated. As a father, I am the person who pays the bills and the 'answer man' for everybody else's problems." As a woman, you might say, "I am a mother, a cook, a wife, a career woman, and a lover. What have I really done in life that has truly made *me* happy? I've sacrificed so that everyone else can have. At work, I conform to what 'they' want me to be and at home I conform to—and accept the responsibility of—being a good little wife. Man, I don't know if I can continue to 'play the role.' I really need to get my freak on!"

"My intimate time is not what it used to be. The sheets are turning into a 'sham.' There are over 101 sexual positions, and I think my mate and I are 99 short. I want to feel like Captain Kirk from the movie 'Star Trek.' I want to seek out strange new adventures and boldly go where no one has gone before. I want to make such a noise that Scottie would have to 'beam us up.' 'Captain, we can't take it anymore! Ah, ah, ah, we're already up to position #101 ... If we keep this up, we are going to blow!' 'Scottie, cool your engine off .. change to position #99 and steady as you go.'" In these examples, the couple is suffering from an acute case of *"needing to get your freak on!"*

You are a happily married man or woman. You love your spouse, your life, and your position in the community. Despite all of this, something seems to be missing. So you buy that sports car you've always dreamed of and now you are chasing 21-year-old girls. As a woman, you, too, feel "Young and Restless," "Bold and Beautiful." So you cut your hair, shorten your dress, and have an affair with a 21-year-old man from the "Daisy Hill Stud Farm." The problem here, too, is described as another severe case of "needing to get your freak on."

Getting your freak on is a popular expression of the '90s. This expression means bringing out the wild, crazy, uninhibited, adventurous side of you . . . or doing something that you have always dreamed of. For a relationship to truly last and become emotionally and physically fulfilling, each person, at some point in time, must be allowed to "get their freak on!"

Getting your freak on occurs in many forms. When it comes to sex and getting your freak on, you first begin with commitment and communication. To really get your freak on requires emotional security. In every woman there is a "hot and sexy 'diva'" waiting to be released. But unfortunately, so many men are not taught to communicate what they enjoy sexually.

Another form of getting your freak on is to be totally alone. This treasure is lost once you are married, but if you have a house with a basement, "camp out" there for a day or two and listen to some old music. For a man, getting his freak on could be going to the Super Bowl or NBA Championship, or playing golf, tennis, basketball, or going fishing, etc.

For a married woman, it's your turn to "freak." Take that exotic vacation you've always dreamed of. If you and your husband can afford it, buy that dream house, or at least put a little away each month towards your dream. Go on that shopping spree or change your hairstyle. Lose weight or add to those diamonds on your wedding ring. Check into a Ritz hotel under an alias. Spoil yourself rotten with a massage, exotic perfume, or a mud bath, and then have your husband meet you there under an assumed name. Then you are free to have an affair with "another man"—your husband!

For me, getting my freak on is jumping on a plane and flying to Cartagena, Colombia, in South America. Cartagena is the oldest city in Colombia. In fact, it is about 2,000 years old. It's a city that time and modernization forgot. Cartagena is known for the most beautiful, exotic, and friendly women in the world. In fact, the ratio of men to women is about 25 to 1. Down there, a man is treated like a king! I love just sitting under a palm tree with my pen and paper, fantasizing and enjoying the scenery and being pampered. My nights are filled with the sounds of waves crashing and singing and dancing on the beach. My days are spent watching "string bikinis."

But you know what is good and healthy about getting your freak on? You want to freak only every now and then, and only temporarily. When that "bad girl" or "bad boy" side of you is satisfied, you are ready to come back to reality and start another day for a few more dollars. You will be ready to listen to "Mommy, stop Mike from pulling my hair!" "I'm hungry!" "I have a cold" or "Honey, what's for dinner?" As you sit at the table with the baby in your arms and return from "Fantasy Land," you can look at each other with naughty glances and think to yourself, "My wife (or husband) is a real freak!"

## The "Wild Thing" Helper
## What to Do When Getting "His" Freak on Is Turning "You" Off

In the '90s, men put a great emphasis on sex. And we all have those "naughty" thoughts, "special treats," or fantasies that turn us on. But what do you do when your mate's "turn-on" is your "turn-off?" For example, bondage, anal sex, whipping, orgies, menage-a-trois (sex with two women simultaneously), or dressing up in your "undies," bra, lingerie, or others?

1. First of all, keep an open mind. You never know if you'll like it unless you first try it. Sexual fantasies are normal, and variety is the spice of life. Now, what is "abnormal" or "perverted" is an individual call or "comfort zone." So don't be afraid to be bold and daring.

2. Reinforce to your mate that you want to fulfill his sexual needs, but be honest by communicating any "reservations" or personal problems associated with fulfilling his desires.

3. Ask for and suggest alternatives.

4. Stay within your "comfort zone."

5. Create and perform your own sexual fantasies.

6. Reserve certain fantasies or sexual acts for special occasions: week-ends, birthdays, anniversaries, holidays, vacations, etc.

7. Always practice safe sex.

8. For any new sexual act, communicate any pain or discomfort you feel. Never let his pleasure be your pain.

9. Don't ever feel that your relationship is based totally on sex. If he leaves you just because you refuse to comply with a certain sexual act, then it's "hasta la vista, Baby." It's good to know up front where you stand.

10. If your mate continues to insist on performing his sexual fantasy, talk dirty to him and, in the heat of making love, tell him to imagine doing that very thing to you.

If getting your freak on is turning your man off, apply these same rules to yourself and always keep in mind that the human mind can conjure up some wild and crazy things and certain fantasies should be only fantasies and nothing else.

## Breaking up Is Hard to Do, Scary to Do, and What Should You Do?

It's 3:00 in the morning, and all through the house, not a creature is stirring, not even a mouse. Your job is "tired," and your "boss" is a "louse"... But a "girl got to do what a girl got to do"... 30 years to go on your cute little house... when suddenly, the telephone rings, your heart pounds with fear—could it be the "boogie man?" You wonder if he's here!

Hello, hello, you say, and no one answers, but you know someone's there because you hear heavy breathing on the phone. You hang up, but just when you're about to "count sheep," the phone rings again. You answer, yelling, "I don't know who's playing this sick joke, so you'd better answer before I call the cops!" Before you can finish, a quivering voice answers on the other end... a voice you have known and been annoyed by so many times. It's your ex-boyfriend. He blurts out, "Melody, I still love you. I can't sleep, eat, or think since we broke up three years ago."

Now you become annoyed. "Michael, it's 3:15 in the f-----g morning. What we had is over. It's adios! Hasta la vista, Baby! Vamos! Tired! Worn out, stale! Our relationship had gotten like Friday the 13th, part 26—old, worn out, little imagination, no excitement, and another 'rerun.'"

"But Melody," the voice interrupts, "I can change!"

You continue, "Michael, it's been three years since we broke up. Go on with your life! Get over it. Our love has gotten old—it lost the 'Yabba Dabba Doo.'"

Michael shouts, "If I can't have you, nobody else will either. I know where you live. I know where you work. When you least expect it, 'Ms. Thing'... ha ha ha... You'll be sorry!"

This story is just one of many about situations women encounter from the "stalker" or "obsessed" file. In fact, this is one of the biggest dangers women will encounter when playing the dating game. Just as important as it is in beginning a relationship is ending it on a positive note.

1. *Be honest from the beginning* with someone you date. If the relationship is friendship only, let them know it.

2. *Never—repeat, NEVER—have a man other than your husband paying your bills or living expenses.* Remember, those who have the gold make the rules. And if he's paying your bills, then he feels the relationship is over when he says that it is over.

3. If a relationship was a one-night stand, make it clear that you don't want it to go any further.

4. Never embarrass or belittle a man in public. Men have large and fragile egos. Nothing will turn a timid, sweet man into a "maniac" like this will.

5. Never break up in the "heat" of anger. Break up only when you are both "sane" and level-headed.

6. When you see that "ex" out, never put on an Academy Award-winning performance with your new love. For example, "This is Bob, a doctor, lawyer, or athlete" and then start "pawing" all over him. Men can't stand this one. Think how you would feel if someone did this to you.

7. Try to be his friend. Never say anything derogatory about him to his friends.

8. Never stay in a bad relationship until something better comes along, then coldly "dump" your man.

9. Never ever go for the jugular when you break up by telling a man he is "impotent" or lousy in bed. This is one of those "permanent damage," dangerous, "I will get even" areas.

10. If you can't be friends with your "ex," then cut off all types of communication completely. This includes telephone calls, cards, letters, smoke signals, Morse Code, and the "Psychic Hot Line."

It might be harsh, but at least you will live to get over it!

## What to Do When You Are Left Barefoot, Broke, and Pregnant

Your man walks in one day, dressed in his Hugo Boss suit and flashing that million dollar smile, a smile you know only too well will cost you about $10,000. "Out of the blue," he looks at you, scanning you from head to toe, and says arrogantly, "Brenda, I want out!"

Shocked and bewildered, you respond, "You what?!"

As he looks at you with disgust, he repeats, "I want out. I'm not happy anymore. I am not happy with you, and I have outgrown our marriage. Look at you, Brenda. You let yourself go to waste. You've blown up like a balloon. You have no ambition, and I am ashamed to take you around my friends in my profession."

"What the hell do you mean, Roger? I can't believe you are saying these cruel things to me, especially after I sacrificed and worked night and day for eight long years to put you through medical school. Now you're on your feet, making a few dollars. You made me quit the two jobs I had, believing all of your dreams and promises. Now for eight years of marriage, and eight years of sacrificing, this is what it boils down to?"

"Brenda, please don't make it more difficult than it has to be. We have nothing left to hold on to. You can have the car and the apartment. I just want out."

"Roger, how can you be so uncaring and insensitive? I believed in you. I trusted you. I gave up so much for 'us,' and all I was really doing was fattening up a frog for a snake. I can see it clearly now. From the start, you saw a 'meal ticket,' a 'bank' to finance your dream, a warm body to lie with and a 'Motel 6' to lie in! Now, after eight years, I am left with nothing—barefoot, broke, and pregnant."

"Pregnant? What do you mean?"

"Roger, haven't you noticed the weight I've been putting on? The morning sickness? My mood swings? You told me when you finished med school that we would start a family. That's why I've blown up like a balloon. Didn't it occur to you? Aren't you supposed to be the doctor?"

"Baby, the last thing I need is kids. I've got my career to think about. I thought you were on the pill. Baby, I'm sorry, but I don't have time to hang around and be a 'daddy.'"

"What?! You lied to me, used me. I can't believe you're saying this to me. Okay, fine, Roger," she sobs. "If you want to leave, leave! I don't need you. You were a 'liability,' not an 'asset.' So let the door hit you where the Good Lord split you. By the way, Mr. M.D., that Hugo Boss suit—please lay it on the table. Those shoes—please put them back in the box. That Polo shirt—please hang it neatly in the closet. You can keep that T-shirt, that's yours. But leave those silk boxer shorts and get the 'holey' drawers you had on when I met you. Now, good-bye!"

This is probably the worst situation any good-hearted, trusting, loving woman can find herself in. Yes, it sounds like a topic fit for the "Oprah Winfrey" show, but it is all too real!

Many women find themselves in this position after years of marriage, living together in a normal relationship, or so much in love with a man that they are totally consumed with that other person. In order to make it over this hump, there are two areas I must address: (1) What to do when you are caught up in this situation, and (2) How to avoid it from the start.

How *not* to get caught barefoot, broke, and pregnant:

1. Have some type of degree or job skills. *Never ever be totally dependent on a man.* I don't care how much money he has or how good the dreams he's selling you sound. Remember, it's a thin line between love and hate. When the relationship goes sour, mates want to hurt each other. If you have nothing but him, you're out of luck. Even if you are a housewife, have something going for yourself. Seek some type of job training, if not just for a selfish reason, but for the reason that something could happen to him and you would have to take charge. In the '90s, you must have skills. The next time your girlfriend brags, "My man takes care of me," shake your head and tell her, "You poor fool!"

2. Get your own, have your own, and you'll never have to worry about being alone.

3. If he starts abusing you physically or emotionally, start putting some "nuts" away for a blizzard. Now, this is the only time I will advise you to have a "secret" bank account—if a man is physically or emotionally abusing you. Once it starts, it usually never stops. Since he can't stop, you must first pause, be cautious, let your money build up—then GO!

4. Always listen to how he talks—listen to the pronouns he frequently uses: "I" or "me" instead of "we" or "us." Sometimes a person will tell you what they are thinking before they drop the bomb on you . . . so listen up!

5. Don't put yourself in the "poor house" from the start, so someone else can live in a mansion.

If it's too late for a sermon, and you need a quick solution, here's what you should do if you are already barefoot, broke, and pregnant:

1. Realize and accept in your mind that the relationship is over. Don't hang on. What do you have to hang on to? Nothing! Your man has told you he wants out, he has someone else, and he does not respect you. You have nothing left to build on. Running after him will only make it worse. Don't ever give a man the chance to have his cake and eat it, too. "Your relationship, from the start, was a misunderstanding between two fools." Now don't keep on being a fool. I realize that you are pregnant and your child will always keep that man in your life, and that man will forever be a part of you. Your first obligation is to yourself and that unborn child. In order to support

both, let's first get your emotional and financial game together. First of all, let's start with the emotional. Read Philippians 4:13, which says, "I can do all things through Christ who strengthens me." You need to leave what is seen out and go to what is unseen—prayer changes everything! Talk to your girlfriend, family, minister, etc. You need the support. Next, increase your job skills. You may not have a degree or specialized training, but right now you need some money, and you need it fast. Hopefully, your family can help you out until you get on your feet. But just in case they are in the "I told you so" corner, then we go to game plan #2:

2. *Adapt, Improvise, and Overcome.* Take a job at night so your days are free to interview. Cut out all unnecessary expenses. For once in your life, you are investing in *YOU!* When you look good, you feel good. When you go on interviews, have "the world is mine" glow, not the "I'm so broke I can't pay attention" look. You are what you present to others. There are good sales jobs that you will be perfect for. Tell your boss you need to work. It's amazing what a little honesty will do.

Now that you are employed, stay in the Bible. You need to keep that strong spiritual base. Avoid negative people and girlfriends coming across with that, "Girl, I told you not to do it" garbage. *You will hurt, you will cry, and you will want to go back!* In fact, the two most painful things in the world are a toothache and a broken heart. But don't give in—stay strong! You will want to do a drive-by, bust a cap on him, or send the hitmen over, but chill—do nothing. You see, *the best revenge is to live well.* Oh, he's going to be back, but go on with your life. Put him and the experience in the class of "Education and Stupidity." Right now, it's about you and that child. When you get a little money, pay your bills, but pay yourself first. Call all of your creditors, give all of the "bulldogs" just a little until you get on your feet.

## Divorce!
## "Celebration" or "Sadness"
## Knowing When . . . The Time to Dissolve a Partnership

"Her 'prying' family broke up our marriage!"

"I left because we could no longer communicate."

"That back-stabbing friend of mine came between us. She had her eyes on my man all the time."

"He suddenly changed on me. I didn't know who he was anymore!"

What all these statements have in common is: They are all reasons for a "failed" marriage, or a divorce. When it comes to a divorce, honestly speaking, the only people who can actually break up, dissolve, or resolve a marriage are the two people involved. It's obvious if you find your mate attractive, someone else will as well. Who would want a mate that someone else didn't find attractive?

Have you sometimes wondered why some marriages seem to be "made in Heaven" and last a lifetime, while others fail from the start? More importantly, have you ever wondered why your marriage failed, especially when you have tried so hard? No, there is nothing wrong with you for being in love and choosing someone you thought would make a good and solid partner. Sometimes two people are simply not right for each other from the start, and relationships can even drift apart. Marriage is just like owning a business. It is very demanding, and you have to work at it so that it can grow and develop. You and your "partner" hope to stay together (i.e., the "company") until retirement or, in this case, until "death do you part." When people are married 50 years, they choose their "partner" for the growth and not the "perks"—money, beautiful homes, status, travel, etc. They choose a partner or company that will provide stability and growth potential. Oh, sure, these "50 yearers" could have been on the "fast track" and could have gone for the "perks," but usually this choice leads to a "high marriage turnover" rate, and they are always reviewing a "new applicant." Their business philosophy is, "What can they bring to the partnership, rather than what they can get."

As their little partnership grows, what started off as something like "sexual harassment" or "the hots for each other" quickly cooled down and matured into a lasting friendship. Many hours of overtime are accumulated in trusting, talking, honesty, and learning to forgive and forget. As a result, you feel you've done all of this and your "partnership" and present day company still have to be dissolved in divorce court? Then pat yourself on the back! You just got rid of a "liability," rather than an "asset." Your "partnership" was doomed from the start! Hallelujah! It's party time . . . bring on the champagne! Go, Baby! Go, Baby! Go, Baby!

## "Paying Rent On" or "Leasing" Your Lover!

Today, women are some of the biggest "movers and shakers" in America. Many of them head major corporations and are now demanding and making top salaries. Oh, yeah, "you've come a long way, Baby!" And men everywhere salute you on your accomplishments. Now, with so many single and "high-powered" women available who are getting paid, the roles have now reversed. Whereas men traditionally took care of the "delicate women," some women are now taking care of their "big, strong men." Here are some of the reasons women gave for "paying rent on" or "leasing" their lover:

1. I don't want to be lonely.

2. He's so "fine," and I don't want to lose him.

3. There is a shortage of quality men, and my biological clock is ticking away.

4. The less time he has to work, the more time he can spend with me and the kids!

5. I make more money, but it's all going in the same pot.

6. What's mine is his, and vice-versa.

7. You get what you pay for!

8. A man is a dog, and my money keeps him on a "leash." He might wander a little bit, but other women will see my "collar" and send him back home to me.

9. He's a great lover!

10. I finally got him where I can "dress him up" and take him to the White House . . . and I don't have any time left to bring in a "rookie."

A woman should never sell herself short or become a financial convenience regardless of how lonely she feels or because of the shortage of available men. Remember, money can't buy happiness, and money surely won't make a man love you. The only thing you may be doing is "fattening up a frog for a snake." If you are a good woman and willing to give your love "unconditionally," that is the only "asset" you need and should use to get and keep a man.

## "Playing it Hard..."
## How to Get Your "Macho Man" to Talk

Now the problem is that from the cradle, parents—especially fathers—teach their sons that "little boys don't cry," or "stop crying and be a man," and "that really didn't hurt, little Johnny, did it?" As a result, men are taught to hide their true feelings and emotions. In school, it became even worse, because peer pressure takes over. If you were rough and tough, you got the girl. If you were weak and sensitive, you got a problem! With all of these years of socialization and environmental conditioning, your man is unable to be as expressive as a woman might like. And women can now see why their men can't shed a few honest tears. You can see now, perhaps, why a man "plays it hard."

How do you get this "iceberg" to thaw out?

1. Tell your man all the positive things you like about him and about your relationship.

2. Tell him your definition of "masculinity," e.g., according to your definition, "real men" cry and show feelings.

3. Get him to trust you more. Reveal something to him about yourself that you never shared with anyone else.

4. Get involved in most of the things he likes to do, regardless of how trivial.

5. Always pay attention to his needs: If he's under a lot of stress, greet him with a smile, or a kind word.

6. Reinforce to him the things he is doing correctly.

7. Allow him "cave time" (the time he withdraws into himself with his thoughts and feelings).

8. Find other things to occupy your time when he is in his "cave time."

9. Never become defensive when he is in his "cave time." It's only temporary.

10. Once he figures out a solution to his problem, then allow him time to re-establish communication with you.

## Why the Beautiful Girls Are All Alone and "The Girl Next Door" Is Seldom at Home!

The problem is that overly beautiful women are thought to be "fantasies" to most men. But one thing about dating or marrying a "fantasy"—oftentimes, once you wake up or once the ring is placed on her finger, your fantasy quickly turns into a nightmare. Why?

1. Her ego is sometimes "out of control."

2. You'll never feel secure with her.

3. She turns into a $100,000 Mercedes—looks good, but requires high maintenance.

4. You'll never know whether you are buying her, leasing her, or putting her on layaway.

Sometimes, beauty and brains don't come as a "package deal." In a woman, intelligence is everything, especially for a mover and shaker man of the '90s. Men want more than "Baby, you just look pretty tonight and let me do the talking. Now, listen to the plan . . . if someone asks you a question, smile, give me a sign, and I will answer it for you, okay?"

On the other hand, every woman is beautiful. Make no mistake about that. If you are one of the lucky ones who's been told all your life, "It's your world," "You're so fine," "You're all of that," make sure you have the personality, charm, attitude, and intelligence to go with it. And then you will become "all of that."

## Getting over a Broken Heart

"In the game of love, no one is immune from a broken heart." It can happen to the best of us. Just when you think you are winning is usually the very time a "cutie" or "hunk" comes along and "rocks your world," bursts your balloon, drops you like a hot potato, or takes the wind out of your sails. Before you know it, your perfect "stats" are blown and now you are spending hundreds of dollars calling the "Psychic Hotline."

I must admit, getting even like Rambo would certainly make you feel better, but that is not the way to truly get over a broken heart. Check out these helpful hints:

1. In order to get over the hurt, you must first feel the hurt. Don't be afraid to cry. You are a human being with feelings. Don't try to be anything else but human. When you are alone, let it out—feel the pain. Cry!

2. Don't return to the dating game until you are emotionally in control.

3. Satisfy your curiosity by finding out why your mate dumped you. If it's constructive criticism, and you feel that you should change, do so. Make sure you want to change, not change to please someone else.

4. Never get involved with someone new on the rebound. If you feel you must date, be honest from the start.

5. Once your mate tells you it's over, accept it. Start the healing process then. Put it in your mind that he or she is no longer a part of your life. Do not try to contact them again . . . let me repeat this one: **Do not try to contact them again**—in any way, shape, or form. That means no

telephone calls, no letters, no riding by their house, sending them smoke signals, faxes, contact on the Internet, calling Mrs. Rudolph—the "Voodoo" lady, burning incense or roots to invoke their essence. Let it go—move on. It did not work, and any further communication will only feed their ego or possibly put you in a position in which you can be used or treated with disrespect.

6. Intimacy ends with the relationship. With a woman, head, heart, and body are usually a "package deal." Often, men may not want the commitment or relationship *but still want the intimacy*. All physical contact should stop once the relationship is over. If not, you will always be on an emotional roller-coaster ride. It's true, you can find good sex anywhere... but a mate who makes love to your mind and respects your feelings is priceless.

7. Once you decide to date, watch out for "Mr. Smooth" who seems an easy "prey." For example, you take a vacation to some exotic island when suddenly the "island Romeo" sees you, walks over to you, and speaks to you with his island accent, "Hey, Chocolate Girl, why are you crying your eyes out in the land of love? What's wrong with you, Girl? You should be running naked, as free as a bird, with the wind blowing in your hair. What a weave, Girl. Free yourself, let the wind blow through your scalp. What? Your man dumped you? What is wrong with him? Is he on dope? Or dog food? Is he blind, crippled, crazy, or have cataracts? You're a beautiful girl. You have big, pretty eyes, luscious lips; in fact, your soup coolers (lips) are so big and pretty, you could probably French-kiss a moose. Come here, Girl. Let me give you a big wet one." Smack, smack! "Now come on back to my hut and enjoy

some Reggae while I dip your feet in honey and suck on your toes!" As I said, stay away from the shark who seems like a minnow drowning in a sea of love.

8. Relieve some stress by working out. Always try to keep your body in great "work-it-baby" shape. The health spa is also a great place to meet a potential mate.

9. Occasionally you will have flashbacks, especially when listening to the radio. So don't hate the disc jockey when he plays records like, "Who's Loving You?" "When A Man Loves A Woman," "Ain't No Woman Like the One I Got," "Always and Forever," "Distant Lover," "I Want You Back," "Ain't No Use in Going Home," "Jodie Got Your Girl and Gone." Please, don't blow up the local radio station. It's only a coincidence that the disc jockey is playing these records when you and your mate have broken up. Just maintain your composure. You will get stronger as time passes.

10. Don't be afraid to talk it over with a level-headed close friend, not the "all the men are dogs" friend. This kind of friend is the one who can't get a man, let alone keep one!

Here are a few character flaws that will certainly get you dumped:

1. Excessive jealousy.

2. Abusiveness—physical or emotional.

3. Annoying habits like drugs or alcohol.

4. Negativity.

5. No sense of humor.

6. Letting yourself go physically, especially if you were health-conscious to begin with. A mate who truly loves you will accept the extra weight, but still you want to give them something to work with . . . the same thing that it took to get your baby hooked is the same thing it will take to keep them.

7. Smothering your mate or being around them constantly—or worse, "under" them.

8. Infidelity or lies.

9. No ambition.

10. Inability to hold a steady job.

So, if you are getting over a broken heart, don't worry. Everything happens for a reason. If you were at fault, learn from your mistakes. If you've done everything you can to make someone else happy, who's the fool? Them or you? Believe me, you'll find another. And when you do, that new love will recognize you as the precious diamond that you are.

*My Soul Mate*

## Conclusion

We have explored every situation imaginable a woman will encounter in dating, relationships in the '90s, and marriage.

You should now feel confident that, not only do you have the necessary tools to get and keep your mate "trained, whipped, faithful, and on a leash," but also you are an expert in:

1. Playing the dating game,

2. Where to find a good man,

3. Choosing a husband,

4. What makes a man fall in love,

5. How to get a man to the altar quick, fast, and in a hurry,

6. The appropriate time for sex,

7. How—and when—to use sex as a weapon,

8. How to tell if your man is cheating,

9. How to quench the thirst for an old flame, and

10. How to get a 50-year warranty with your marriage.

You should also have learned by now that dating, love, and relationships are not complicated at all. People make them complicated. If you think you are headed for a heart break, always remember, trust your "gut" instincts. "If it looks like a duck, walks like a duck, and talks like a duck, then it is probably a duck!" At this point, get out of the game. Take your ball and bat and go home, "cool out" awhile, and don't let anyone else play on your field!

After you've had time to clear your head and think things over, you're about ready to return for the "second half." In your next relationship, or even in your current relationship, do something that is totally against playing the dating game in the '90s. That unspeakable thing, or "monkey wrench" that you are about to throw into the dating game is called honesty—being yourself and most of all, being considerate of the other person.

## CHAPTER II

**FOR MEN ONLY**
Introduction

Now, before a man starts dating or thinking about putting a woman of the '90s on a "leash," he must first learn what makes her "tick" or, in some cases, "explode!"

Now, understanding a woman is perhaps the 9th wonder of the world. Many books have been written on this delicate subject, and to be perfectly honest, I had to study her for three years and interview about 3,000 of them just to feel comfortable writing this book. After all that has been written and said, men are still puzzled. Man has invented atomic bombs, gone to the moon, lived under water, survived years of drought, hurricanes, famine, and gone where few men have gone before. And yet, with all the advanced science we have available at our fingertips, men still can't figure out and predict with 100% accuracy the behavior of the complex being called "woman!" On Monday, she can be as sweet as a vintage wine, deadly as a cobra on Tuesday, happy-go-lucky on Wednesday, angry because she's angry on Thursday, "you're an insensitive jerk" on Friday, "Darling, I miss you" on Saturday, and "I'm not in the mood" on Sunday.

How do we understand such a complex being of such "chameleon" behavior? Rule #1 is that you can't group all women into one single category. So let me rephrase everything and say: To understand *your* woman and to find out what makes *her* tick, you need to take a ride home with her and check out her parents to see how she was reared. Now it's true, "The acorn doesn't fall far from the tree!" In order to better understand your mate, you first need to know what "seeds" or, in some cases, "fertilizer," was first planted into her head. If her mother was happy in her marriage and her relationship, and she was emotionally secure, overall your mate will have a pleasing personality, a healthy perception of relationships, and no "hangups" about the opposite sex.

But regardless of how your woman was reared, and her ethnic background notwithstanding, there are common bonds that all women share. If you keep the following in mind, *you, too, can unlock the 9th wonder of the world and predict your woman with 99% accuracy:*

1. A need for security, emotionally and financially. A need to be part of something or belong to something or someone. Even when you hear a woman make a statement like, "I don't have time for a man or marriage . . . I'm married to my work"—there is still the need to be part of something. But if you come into her life with the right "program" and credentials, you can quickly break her defenses down.

2. Women are generally stronger emotionally than men. They can certainly handle more stress. But on the other hand . . .

3. Women are a "push over" when it comes to attention, affection, a great smile, a child, a puppy, a teddy bear, flowers, nice shoes, a well-dressed man, a man who smells nice, a convertible car, flowers sent to her job, a man bragging to his friends about her, a picnic, a man agreeing with her, a man who loves children, a man with a nice body and a tight butt, and also she's a push over for a man who sings to her—even off-key!

4. A woman will have mood swings. Because of her biological make-up and variation of hormone levels, her moods will also change. Be patient when she says things like "I'm angry because I'm angry," or "I hate you but I love you" . . . it will soon pass!

5. Women can go longer than men without sex. Sex is emotional to a woman, not always physical. If you can make love to a woman's mind and heart first, then you're in there!

6. Women enjoy sex just as much as a man, although they can go longer without it. Women can have three to five orgasms in a single love session compared to one time for a man. Women also fantasize about men and think what it would be like! That "what it would be like" could be you!

7. A woman can check out a man physically in one quick glance—from his shoes, socks, eye color, clothes he's wearing, and even tell which loop he missed putting his belt through on his trousers.

8. Women determine a man's success by the little things: quality shoes, quality clothes, and the quality of his living conditions.

9. The biggest turn-on to a woman is laughter. Have a sense of humor like Martin Lawrence—"You So Crazy!" Eddie Murphy—"Get the F-ck Out of Here!" or Richard Pryor—"The Girl Put a 'Moe-Joe' on Me. Call Mrs. Rudolph." Then you've got her hooked!

10. Women are taught that men should have just as much or more than them. Notice, I said "taught." To a woman, the only acceptable excuse for having less, especially if you're in your 30s, is that you're recently divorced or recovering from a business disaster. But if you can get next to her head and heart, that "fertilizer" her mother and friends put in her mind won't even matter.

11. Never ever call a woman of the '90s a bitch, because once you do, you've blown the game completely. The only comeback afterwards is hitting the Lotto and sharing your winnings with her. But once she gets that, she's still out of there.

12. Treat a woman well emotionally, and be there for her. She'll never leave.

13. Occasionally the woman of the '90s is going to "try" her man just to see how much he can "stand" and to see how much she can get away with. Don't explode. Just be polite and "kill" her with kindness.

14. It doesn't take a woman all day to get a "cut," "shampoo," or a "curl." The beauty parlor is where women go to "bond," catch the latest gossip, latest fashion news, and can even get the 411 on her man. If your "stuff" is "loose," you will certainly be busted.

15. Women are just like the FBI They seldom come at you with just a "little" something or something that you can "squirm" your way out of. Just like the FBI, they watch you for a minute, let everything build up, and then when you least expect it, they walk in and start the "bust" with

times, dates, places, faces, and have a list of witnesses. Your "indictment papers" or, in this case, your divorce papers, are already typed and hand-delivered, with no "scene" or "drama." And just like an FBI "bust," your reaction is usually the same: "It wasn't me!" or "Can we make a deal?" or "Let's work something out!"

16. As a man, you will have to "check" your woman occasionally. But never do it with anger or violence. Do it with style. "Baby, you know that you are wrong . . . you know that I love you . . . and the person that I fell madly in love with is not the person I see now. We are a team. Team members fight together, not against each other. Now sweetheart, when I return, the person I see now, I want her to be gone and the person I love to return. Here's a number where I can be reached, just in case you or the kids need me." Then turn and walk out. Your woman is "checked" with style. And even though you both wear the pants, the real man has just stood up!

You know, women of the '90s are not difficult to deal with or to understand. A woman of the '90s doesn't mind being a "follower," but *she just wants to make damn sure the man she is following first qualifies to lead her.*

In order for a man to play "The Dating Game" successfully, he too must be up on his game, learn to recognize the game, and if he's losing, learn how to carry the game into "overtime." All through this chapter, I'll reveal how to read the opposite sex—their game plans, how to "blow their game," and when it's time to leave the game completely.

## Running up the Price of "Coochie"
## The Price Tag for a Woman Has Gotten "Outrageous!"

You're out at a hot night spot and a "10" walks in the door. Not only does "Baby" have "back," but "front," legs, intelligence, and the looks. Men immediately begin "checking her out." She sees that it's "her" world and decides she'd better start choosing. Before you know, "Willie Lunchmeat" sends her a bouquet of freshly cut, long-stemmed roses imported from Rome, Italy, and leaves the price tag on them. "Paymaster," not to be outdone, sends his "gold card" over with a note saying, "Just the two of us in Paris, France." "Sammy Sausagehead" sees her smiling and decides he'd better join in the "bid" and immediately jumps into his $250,000 Lamborghini, pulls up in front of her, throws the door in the air, and says, "Hey, Baby, this is definitely not your father's Oldsmobile!" By now, "Larry Lump Lump" is green with envy. He "rolls" up to her in his vintage Rolls Royce, looks at "Sammy Sausageheads'" Lamborghini, and says, "Didn't Chrysler just buy Lamborghini?" At this point, "Johnny the Jock" pulls up in a two-block stretch limousine, diamond in the back, moon roof, sun roof, star roof, sky roof, and an opening just in case someone wants to "eat a Baby Ruth." Chauffeuring "Johnny the Jock" around is a Japanese trained in Kung Fu and an Italian cook named Guiseppi. He then steps out of his Limo with genuine crocodile shoes (you know they are real crocodile because one of the crocodiles just bit "Larry Lump Lump" on the butt), and all the other "bidders" stop bidding because they know they all have a willing mind, but their pockets are too "light" behind. "Johnny the Jock" wins the bid, and the girl, and they both live happily ever after in his $10 million estate.

Men, men, it doesn't take "all of that" to get a woman in the '90s. The only thing you're doing is "swelling a woman's head," making it bad for the "real men," and running the price of "coochie" sky-high!

Always remember, if your girl is more expensive than your car note, or more expensive than your house note, it's better to let *her* get "repossessed" or "foreclosed" on! But on the other hand, if you must have her, save up enough money, put her on "layaway," arrange a payment plan, or just get her out in the Fall!

## How to Make Your Wife Your Girlfriend, the Other Woman, and Your Chick on the Side

It's 2:00 a.m., and two mysterious figures pull up to an "out of the way" motel on the other side of town. Both are wearing dark trench coats. A scarf covers the woman's face, and she keeps her face low to further conceal her identity. She then greets her lover, who is wearing a hat pulled down on his face like Humphrey Bogart. They meet in the lobby.

As the woman pretends to use the telephone, the man walks up to the hotel desk and asks the clerk for his reserved room. He signs his name as "Bill Jones." The clerk looks at him and smiles. You see, every six months for the past ten years, *Bill Jones has brought his wife and his "chick on the side" to the same motel.* To make matters worse, his "chick on the side" knows his wife, and he knows her husband like his own name. He and his mistress are both respectable members of society with three kids at home. The man then sticks out his chest and gives the desk clerk a foxy grin. Then he "slithers" up the stairs with a look that says, "I got it going on."

Opening the door to his room, he is once again greeted by his mysterious woman. By now, she is full of desire, lust, passion, and fire. She "paws" him like a wild woman. He picks her up and walks her across the threshold. As they enter the room, they notice the dim lights and romantic music playing in the room. The man then grabs a glass of wine, gives her a sip, and then kisses her passionately. As they rip off their clothes and submerge themselves in the Jacuzzi filled with "Mr. Bubble," they continue to sip the wine and smile at the rose petals scattered on the floor.

Suddenly, someone starts banging on the door. BAM . . . BAM . . . BAM! "Open the door! I know both of you are in there!"

The couple jumps out of the tub and hastily put on bathrobes. As they walk hesitantly toward the door, they tremble in fear. They look through the peephole, but the stranger has made sure to remain obscured. All of a sudden, "guilt" overtakes your "chick on the side" and she starts to sing like a canary. "I knew he would find us! I knew he would come! Bill, it's no use—we are caught, we are 'busted.'" You motion to her to maintain her composure. As the knocks get louder, the voice becomes more demanding. "I know you're in there! Open up! Open up!"

You whisper to each other, "How did your husband find out?" "How did your wife find out?"

The stranger continues knocking on the door. "I know you both are in there! I followed you to your 'den of sin.'" With guilt overtaking you, both of you realize it is hopeless. After ten years of having a "sordid" affair with each other, you knew one day you would get caught. As your mistress gets behind you, you finally open the door, and the "demanding stranger" enters the room. You both burst out laughing at your little game. It is your 16-year-old son! "Mom, Dad," he laughs. "I knew I'd find both of you here." He looks at the two of you standing there, dripping wet, and takes in the romantic atmosphere, and he starts to laugh. "Don't you think you're a little too old to be sneaking around and *having an affair with each other?*"

As you laugh, you ask if everything is okay at home. He replies that it is, and that the reason he came was because he needed $10 to go on a date. You give him the money and quickly get rid of your "unwanted guest." Then you go back to the sordid affair with your wife, who has been *adventurous* enough to be your wife, your girlfriend, your other woman, and your chick on the side!

## When a Woman Wants a Wedding Ring— She's Not "Above" Playing Dirty

Oh, yes! That's right! I said it! When a woman's "biological clock" starts ticking and she's ready for a wedding ring, be warned: *no woman is "above" playing dirty!!*

Now, for a man to be "up on his game," he must be on his toes for the "Wedding Ring Game" . . . here's how it is played:

1. "I'm pregnant."

2. You need to make up your mind whether or not someone else is also "pressuring" her to marry him.

3. She finds your best friend attractive. If she was not involved with you, he would be her second choice. This one also has other variations, like: "Why don't you invite 'Larry' over for dinner? He's so crazy! I like him. I see he's been working out."

4. She refrains from sex for a few days. Then she calls you up and talks dirty to you on the telephone.

5. She invites you over unexpectedly, meets you at the door wearing a sexy negligee—or is completely nude. Then, "out of the blue," she becomes angry and throws you out of the house. Sixty-five percent of men interviewed "went down in flames" with this one.

Now, if #5 fails, she then reaches deep into her "bag of tricks" and says:

6. "If you don't want my love, I might as well give it to someone else. I'm going out by myself tonight." Then she

throws on those pumps or that dress you like so much, winks at you, and walks out the door.

7. She met someone else who is "smarter," better looking, or richer, and the two of them become very close. Of course she is going to tell you her "new lover" is always spending a lot of money on her and wants to take her to some exotic hideaway.

8. "My upbringing will not allow me to continue to be intimate without a commitment."

9. Buy or borrow a wedding ring and tell you another man gave it to her and he's pressuring her to marry him.

10. When all else fails, she gives you an ultimatum. You will not have your cake and eat it too. "You are not going to continue to get the 'milk' free, if you don't 'buy the cow.' Either you marry me, or I'm out of here."

As I said earlier in this chapter, all is fair in love and war. And although these "tricks" are unorthodox and totally against the "rules" of the "game," they have been working for years. So if you don't want to play the game, stay off the field. Get your ball and bat and go home.

On the other hand, even if a woman is not playing fair, you need to be fair because "two wrongs don't make a right."

It is obvious when a woman starts hitting below the belt. She is doing it because she cares about you and wouldn't like anything better than to have a life with you. A woman has to feel that she is not wasting her time. A woman's heart, mind, and body work as a unit. So, when she's giving of herself, this is her greatest gift. When she has to resort to threats and unorthodox "tricks," step aside and let a "good man" who's looking for a "good woman" come in and take over.

## Is it Best to Tell Women the Unfiltered Truth?

*"You can't handle the truth!"* actor Jack Nicholson roared in the movie "A Few Good Men." In fact, 75% of the single and married men interviewed seem to agree with Jack. According to my interviewees, "The truth may set you free, but the truth may also set you up." Why? The men surveyed had this to say:

1. Women are just like a police raid: Anything you say can and will be used against you during an argument or a divorce.

2. What she doesn't know can't hurt her or, in most cases, you!

3. Women want to live a fairy-tale life in which they all live happily ever after.

4. In a similar survey, 70% of the women revealed that their mothers taught them not to tell a man everything.

5. It is best not to let your right hand know what your left hand is doing.

6. A man who says everything he thinks is a fool. If it's not broken, don't try to fix it.

7. You're wrong only if you get caught!

8. She might "forgive," but she will never "forget." And she will never let *him* forget it either!

9. This is real life, not "The Cosby Show." My lady is not like Claire Huxtebel.

10. Women act too much on emotion.

In fact, the things men and women lie about most frequently are:

1. Their financial status.

2. Their marital status—single or married.

3. Where they live.

4. Having an affair with someone else.

5. Their true feelings.

6. Age.

7. Sexual fulfillment.

8. Background—"I'm originally from L.A." or New York or some other "sophisticated" city. Often, they are from "Give Me Bus Fare, Tennessee."

Lies, lies, and more lies cannot produce a healthy relationship. We will all encounter information or news that we can do or live without. But after the shock is over, you will be happy that your mate confessed. Lack of honesty is one of the contributing factors to the high divorce rate. How often have you heard a person say, "I didn't know my mate was like that?" Remember, the truth will definitely set you free, not "set you up." And if a woman "can't handle the truth"—then she is not the one for you anyway!

*Lyrical Lunatic*

## All Kids Are Not like "Bey-Bey's" Kids . . . Dating a Woman with Children

One of the things that most single men will encounter when playing the dating game is single women with children. About a year ago, I was out at a well-known jazz spot in Atlanta. I was at the bar, groovin' to the sounds of Kenny G. Sitting behind me was a woman with the biggest, prettiest brown eyes I had ever seen. I completely turned around and gave her my "Colgate" smile. As she smiled back, I slyly looked down at her calves. Now you know. If a woman has thick calves, she usually has a nice body, nice butt, and developed legs; but if those calves are skinny, let's move on to the next one! Well, anyway, she told me that her name was Angela Williams and that she was a data processor. I then thought to myself, "Hmm, hmmm, she's employed, she's got big, pretty brown eyes, big legs, big hips, she's intelligent, and spiritual, it's all good—no need to waste any more time!" So I said to her, "Angela, let me take you out for a romantic dinner tomorrow night." Stunned at my boldness, she laughed and—surprisingly—agreed. She then gave me her number and address and told me to pick her up about 8:00 the following night.

I arrived at Angela's place at 8:00 sharp. As I checked out her apartment complex, I saw a little girl with braids looking at me from the window, smiling and waving. Then, when I approached the door to go upstairs, two boys, 8 and 10 years old, suddenly came running out, stepping on my crocodile shoes, and knocking me down. I thought to myself, "This neighborhood has a lot of kids." The two boys quickly apologized. Straightening out my clothes, I walked upstairs to Angela's apartment. I rang the doorbell and smiled as Angela appeared. I gave her a hug. Suddenly, the little girl who had been looking out the window smiling and waving came bursting into the room. Angela smiled and said, "This is Maketa, my 6-year-old daughter." I smiled at the little girl and hugged her, thinking to myself, "So Angela has a daughter." As my mind wandered in thought, the doorbell and the telephone rang simultaneously. Angela asked me to get the door while she got the telephone.

At the door, I found that our "intruders" were the same two little boys who had knocked me down earlier. They introduced themselves as "Ricky" and "Ronnie." I then received another "shocker": Angela Williams was also *their* mother! In a daze, I immediately began to think back to our initial conversation. How could someone "hide" three children? Why hadn't she told me about them? Come to think of it, I had never asked her—it simply had never come up. I had been so captivated by her inner beauty, intelligence, and spiritual beauty, and . . . okay, her calves, too! . . . that everything else had seemed unimportant!

As I gazed at the three children who resembled "stepping stones," I thought to myself, "This is not happening to me! I am single, never been married, and have no children. How did I 'hook up' with a sister with 'Bey-Bey' kids?" I knew then how Robin Harris must have felt in the movie, "Bey-Bey Kids" (Robin Harris was a famous comedian, and he met a woman named "Bey-Bey" who had children who were "such terrors" that he decided to call the children "Bey-Bey Kids"). Don't get me wrong—I love kids, and one day I want to have them. But not three right off the bat! You see, my problem at that time was, my friends used to tell me "horror stories" about dating women with children. And the last thing I needed was for Angela and me to one day fall in love, have an argument, and have her kids "gang up" on me, take all my money, send me "packing" back to Alabama, broke with a "whipped butt" with Pampers stuffed in my mouth, riding on the bus with some "now or later" candy stuck in my ears! *No! I don't think so! Brittian doesn't play that!* Angela was cute, sure enough, but she was not "all of that."

Well, anyway, as Angela continued to talk on the phone, those "knucklehead" boys . . . I'm sorry . . . those sweet little "angels" of hers . . . walked over to me and apologized again. I got over my anger immediately as Ricky, the oldest, extended his hand in friendship and said, "Sorry, Mr. Wilder, for stepping on your foot. So you are an author and a businessman, and you deal in international finance?" He continued. "Mr. Wilder, should I invest my allowance or my mom's money in options, or play it safe with penny stocks?"

My mouth flew open. "What?! Where did you learn stuff like that?" I asked Ricky.

"Reading *The Wall Street Journal*. My hero was finance genius Reginald Lewis."

Reginald Lewis was an African-American Wall Street "wizard" who ran the first billiondollar African-American business, "TLC Beatrice Foods." Then Ronnie, the younger brother, walked over to me and said, "I predict that 1997 will be a 'bullish' year for the stock market. That's if the 'Fed' doesn't tighten the Federal Reserve."

I was looking at these two "brainy" kids in amazement as they were telling me things that only skillful investment bankers know. While I lost myself in my amazement, Angela got off the phone with a disappointed look on her face. "Brittian, I have some bad news," she began. "I have to cancel our date because one of the girls at work got sick and I have to go in to take her place." She then asked me the unthinkable. "Brittian, it's too late to find a babysitter. Can you sit the kids for a couple of hours?"

As I looked at those little "roughnecks" . . . sorry again . . . "little darlings" . . . I thought to myself, "Bill Cosby I am not!" Out loud, however, I replied, "But of course, Angela, I'll be happy to!" I then imagined myself being "hogtied" and beaten with a bat by these little "parole potentials" . . . I mean, future leaders of tomorrow.

As Angela left, she said, "Brittian, I promise to make it up to you."

I looked into those big brown eyes, saw the pretty smile, and thought of the big butt, and I remembered the singing trio "Bell, Biv, Devoe," who said, "Never trust a woman with a big butt and a pretty smile." And later I found that to be true. At that moment, however, it was too late. I had committed to being "Bill Cosby" for a couple of hours!

As soon as Angela left, Ricky, the older of the two, immediately took charge. He made sure Ronnie and Maketa did their homework. Then he checked the homework that each of them had done. Next, he made sure the dishes were washed, the windows and doors were locked, and all was safe. He finished his own homework and capped his night off with trying to "map out" his investment strategy with a $5-a-week allowance!

Once everyone had finished his or her homework, we all sat down to watch television until about 10:00 p.m. Ricky then said, "Okay, troops, it's time for bed." He helped Maketa finish braiding her hair, and everyone jumped in the tub. I sat bewildered. I had never seen such well-mannered kids. At once, I felt ashamed of myself for having "stereotyped" all women with children. After their bath, the children put on pajamas. Then Maketa said something that touched my heart. She said innocently, "Mr. Brittian Wilder, for a grown-up, you're not so 'tired' after all." I smiled at her and gave her a hug. She offered me her thumb to suck on and then some of her "now or later" candy. I told her a bedtime story, one from this book, as a matter of fact—the story about my cousin, the ugly duckling who grew up to be a beautiful swan—then we both fell asleep with me holding her tightly and her thumb nestled in my left ear.

It was about 12:15 a.m. when Angela awakened me, smiling and saying, "You need to try this more often! You're a natural!"

I smiled, picked up Maketa and put her to bed, gently kissing her goodnight.

You know, that experience with the "Bey-Bey Kids"... sorry (chuckle) ... Angela's kids ... taught me one thing: the woman of your dreams may not always come in the form of a professional woman with a Ph.D., but rather a plain, everyday woman who is working hard and willing to shower you with L-O-V-E. And in the '90s, you will encounter many women with children. But don't assume just because she has kids, that the kids are like "Bey-Bey's"... Bad to the Bone!

Now, to date a woman with children carries mixed emotions, especially if the man she is dating never had children himself. Just because a woman has children doesn't imply that she is "loose" or not a "morally respectable" girl. Having a child or children could happen as a result of a divorce, mistake, etc. The moral of the story is this: don't be quick to judge. Think of your "bed-hopping" days. Think what would happen if *you* became pregnant as a result of your past conquests. So "chill out" on being Billy Graham.

If you are dating a woman with a child or children, be very considerate of her delicate position. Her time is not all her own. She can't get a babysitter at the drop of a dime and go off to some wild place to act "crazy and silly." Usually, single mothers are very protective of their offspring. It's not you, personally, but children get used to seeing someone and become very attached. The mother just doesn't want the child to get hurt, in the event your relationship doesn't work out.

Once you find out that a woman has a child and that the mother and her child are a "package deal," you can't have one without the other. The child can't just be shipped off to its dad or to boarding school because you can't deal with the situation. If you can't accept the mother *and* the child, you need to be on your "merry way."

The secure woman of the '90s is not looking for a man to help her take care of her children, but rather a good man who will be a positive role model for her offspring. They can usually take care of their youngsters themselves.

Just because a woman has children doesn't make her less sexual or physically desirable. Often women exercise after pregnancy to keep themselves physically and emotionally healthy. So with the women of the '90s, you can't look at them anymore and tell whether or not they have kids!

Children are the "ultimate" thing a woman can offer a man. I also realize that at some point in time, you may want your own child or children. That in itself is not a problem. Make sure, however, that this is clear in the initial stages of the relationship. In a relationship, there is no such thing as "my child" or "your child." It's "our children." You can't treat one child better than you treat another! If you can't think in those terms, it's best once more to be on your "merry way."

## Staying in the "Game"...
## For All the Good Men Who Always Seem to Pick a "Bad" Woman

You're a successful man of the '90s—you've made all the right career choices, right job decisions, and you're now up with the "big boys" playing in the corporate "major league." But when it comes to making the right decision or choosing the right girl, you have slipped from the "majors" all the way down to the "minor league," and you seem to fall for every "curve" that comes your way. If this is you, let's call a quick time-out and go to the dugout and learn to "choose the right ball" so that the next time you are at bat, you can hit a home run!

1. True beauty grows inward and radiates outward.

2. Make sure you both want, and are looking for, the same things.

3. Nobody's perfect. Decide the characteristics that you want most in a woman, and seek out that type.

4. Go to quality places to meet a quality woman.

5. Protect your emotions and your heart. Don't be too quick to fall in love.

6. Impress her with yourself before you start showering her with gifts.

7. Make sure you are "all of that" yourself before you put those standards on someone else.

8. "Water seeks its own level" ... and so should you.

9. Don't always go out looking for a mate. Let them find you!

10. If you're looking for a "perfect woman," remember, she doesn't exist. Look in the mirror—you're not the perfect man!

## "It's Crying Time Again"— and It's Very, Very Masculine

You know, for a man to cry used to be taboo. The only way a man could get away with a good cry was around his mother, but the moment your father, the fellows, or your girlfriend find out about it, you might as well pack your bags and leave town. In fact, as children, men were taught that "little boys don't cry" and "stop crying and be a man!" As we grew older, we stopped crying and tried to act like what society called "being a man." As a result, it led to:

    A. Sensitivity to problems in our relationships.

    B. Confusion about rearing our sons in the '90s.

    C. Emotional stress, anger in our homes.

    D. Arguments, loss of hair.

    E. A shorter life span.

    F. Heart attacks.

Well, I'm proud to announce to men everywhere: "It's crying time again" in the '90s, and it's now in style and very, very masculine. In fact, leading doctors, psychologists, health experts, and most of all, the women of the '90s, have given men the "green light" on shedding a few honest tears. Moreover, women find it sexy, honest, and very masculine.

So, men across America, "it's crying time again." Don't be afraid to shed a few honest tears. I don't know whether or not it's "masculine" to let her see you "sweat," but I know it's very masculine to let her see you cry.

## Got to Have a Roughneck!

Now, what makes a woman want a roughneck? Well, here are the most popular responses women across America gave:

1. Men who are dominant, take charge and can keep them in "check."

2. "Strong" women often run over "weak" men.

3. "Roughnecks" are "real" men. They say what they feel, and they don't compromise. If someone doesn't like it, so what?

4. Roughnecks live on the edge, and some women find it to be a real "turn-on."

5. Roughnecks are wild from the "jump," and lovemaking with them is even wilder.

6. "Good" girls sometimes want to experience a man who's different. "I'm tired of 'pretty boys,' tired of '8 to 4, 9 to 5.' Give me a brother who is a potential '10 to 20' (prison potential), or an 'outlaw.'"

7. You know if someone "challenges you. You know he's 'got your back.'"

8. Roughnecks usually have a lot of women. It boosts your ego to take him away from all the others.

9. If he *does* hit you, it turns you on. (Note: This is not the opinion of the author.)

10. Roughnecks are usually very jealous—"and I love it."

In my survey, only 12% of the women said they had to have a roughneck. But 88% of the women said they still *desire, get turned on by*, and are daily seeking a man who is truly a "gentle man."

## Be Careful What You Ask for . . . You Might Get It!

I was at a popular "hot spot" a couple of week-ends ago, and before you know it, "BAM"—a "Perfect 10" walks through the door! In my mind, she's the one. I begin to see a wife, kids, a station wagon, a dog named "Spot." I ask her out, and after a few dates, I fall in love with her and begin to "wine and dine" her. We take walks in the park. I send her flowers, the works. Soon, after months of trying to win her over, it happens: things start to change. She now wants money for her rent, money for her car, money for clothes, money for hair, her nails, and money just in case she needs money. Shocked and bewildered, I ask myself, "Why did I ever want her in the first place?"

In New York City, a very good friend of mine has her eye on a young stockbroker. He is handsome and charming, and Audrey thinks he is the right mate. After months of wearing perfume, new dresses, and meeting at the "water cooler," he falls in love with her. Before long, "Prince Charming" suddenly turns into "Dr. Jekyll and Mr. Hyde." He becomes possessive, excessively jealous, watching her house every night, and trying to pick her friends for her. Shocked and bewildered, she asks herself, "Why did I ever want him in the first place?"

In Chicago, my friend Bill worked 24 hours a day, seven days a week, for years to become the "branch manager." One day, lo and behold, it happens: he gets the promotion. He's now in the "big leagues." His salary doubles, and so do his responsibilities. He's now under twice as much pressure and constantly argues with his wife, hardly spending any time with the kids.

In all these stories, everyone got what they thought they wanted. In actuality, however, there are three morals to these stories:

1. Be careful what you ask for . . . because you might get it.

2. Sometimes the "hunt" is better than the "kill."

And the one we can all relate to:

3. "Sometimes you want to 'kill' WHAT YOU ONCE WANTED."

## In the Dog House . . .
## Can a Woman Truly Forgive and Forget Infidelity?

In a survey done with 3,000 women across the country, they all agreed, "Trust is the most important thing you can have in any relationship. It takes months and sometimes years to gain it and keep it, but once it is lost, it's hard to get back and oftentimes is never restored." So you're at this point, and it's too late for a sermon. Right now, you need a solution. How can you get back in the good graces of your mate when you have messed up "big time?" Well, this one is going to take time. It will not happen overnight. To understand how she feels, do a role reversal—put yourself in her position.

How would you feel to have your mate share your intimate time with someone else? To be lied to? To build your hopes and dreams with someone and put your trust in someone, only to have it all thrown away for a fling, an ego boost, a one-night stand, or to see whether or not you've still got it, or just to impress the boys? How would it feel to lie next to your mate knowing that they have been with someone else? The special things you shared are no longer special.

If you have kids, it becomes even worse. You want to leave, but you can't. You want to stay, but your pride, ego, and self-esteem will not let you.

How would you feel if someone, even your own mother, told you that your wife was cheating, or no good, and you became angry and called your own mother a "liar?" How would you feel if you loved and believed in someone so much, so deeply, that you might have seen them together and made up every excuse that what you were seeing with your own eyes was not true? How can you look at that person again and let them touch you, knowing that they have given that same affection to someone else?

This might be the '90s, but some mates are from the old school in which "I love you" means "I love you." This is a time when you have to work your way up from a good-night kiss and you sleep on the couch, if you are lucky enough to stay over at all! This is a time when "intimacy" and "commitment" go hand-in-hand, when making love is just what it says—"making love." You feel excited, and you know that she doesn't "do it" with anyone else. It means something. It's the ultimate, the Fourth of July, New Year's Eve, the big countdown, the "ultimate" prize. Now those feelings and the "specialness" are gone. She has been hurt, betrayed, lied to, and made to look like a fool. Now in answering the question "Can a woman truly forgive infidelity?" the answer is "yes," but it won't be easy. It will take a lot of patience. It will take understanding one minute she's happy and another minute she's sad. It will take hugging you on Monday and wanting to hit you on Tuesday. It will take being more "attentive" to her needs and understanding all her pain.

But time has a tendency to heal all wounds. And when it comes to infidelity, this rule is no exception. As time passes, and she sees a "new person" in you, then and only then can a woman truly learn to forgive and forget infidelity.

# CHAPTER III

# AFRICAN-AMERICAN RELATIONSHIPS

## Understanding a Black Man and Black Woman

In order for African-American men and women to be truly happy in a relationship, they must first love and appreciate themselves, appreciate what makes them different, unique, special, and "one of a kind."

Each person must remember: Just as you have been hurt, so has your mate. Come into a new relationship with an open mind, a willingness to communicate, and with renewed excitement. Improve upon that which you can change and accept that which you cannot. Let go of the past, and look forward to the future. Remember: it's a new day, a new mate, a new relationship, and—I hope—a new "you!"

Now, in order for young African-American men and women also to be successful, they, too, must learn to appreciate their counterpart. And in order to prepare and "program" young African-Americans for a healthy relationship, there are a few things every parent should teach their children:

1. *Respect yourself* and others will *respect you*.

2. True beauty begins "inwardly" and radiates "outwardly."

3. Be proud of your full lips, developed legs, and round bottom. They've been in style for years and everybody else is now catching on.

4. "Love" is sometimes a "misunderstanding" between "two fools!"

5. Looks aren't important. Choose a man who will love you, honor you, respect you—and *together* you can build.

6. Premarital sex doesn't make a man love you more, but it does prolong your engagement.

7. "L-O-V-E" and a "J-O-B" is always "a marriage made in heaven!"

8. Too much advertisement "cheapens" the product.

9. Just because a man "flashes" money doesn't mean he has it. All men set aside their "rent money."

10. If he hits you while you're dating, he will hit you while you're married.

11. Make sure he's "out the door" on "strike three!"

12. Make sure your body is not your only claim to fame. What goes up will eventually come down.

13. Beauty is not only "skin deep" but now comes in a bottle.

14. Make your own "success story" instead of always wanting to become part of someone else's.

15. Judge your mate not by what they say or do when the sun is shining, but what they say or do when there's a storm.

16. Be the example to your kid. Take time for them.

17. Know the difference between a "diamond" and a "diamel."

    A. A diamond is rough and can take punishment.

    B. A diamel looks good and can fool anybody—but it's a fake! The moment pressure is put on it, the diamel will break and fall apart.

18. A man wants to marry a woman who believes in God or a higher power.

19. There is no shortage of "good black men," but there is a shortage of Mercedes-driving, Armani suit-wearing, briefcase-carrying, $100,000-a-year making men in the shade of "black."

20. A man is not measured by how many babies he can make, but the number of babies he has made and is taking care of.

21. Respect your black woman. She is the most beautiful woman on earth—everybody else is either trying to look like her or imitate her.

22. If you can honestly say you have done everything to make someone happy, then who is the fool?—Them? Or you?

23. Never come to the "party" with a bag of potato chips and expect to take home steak. Water should seek its own level.

24. If your girl is more expensive than your car note or more expensive than your house note, then it is better to let *her* get "repossessed" or "foreclosed upon."

25. The easiest way to test your relationship is by telling your girl just two simple things:

    A. Baby, I'm broke and I will lose everything that I have,

    or

    B. Baby, I'm in jail and may have to do some "time." In 30 days or less, you will see for yourself what you really have.

26. Give a man emotional support.

27. Stand by your man.

28. You can catch more flies with honey than with vinegar.

29. An investment in your man is an investment in yourself and your future.

30. Always think long-term.

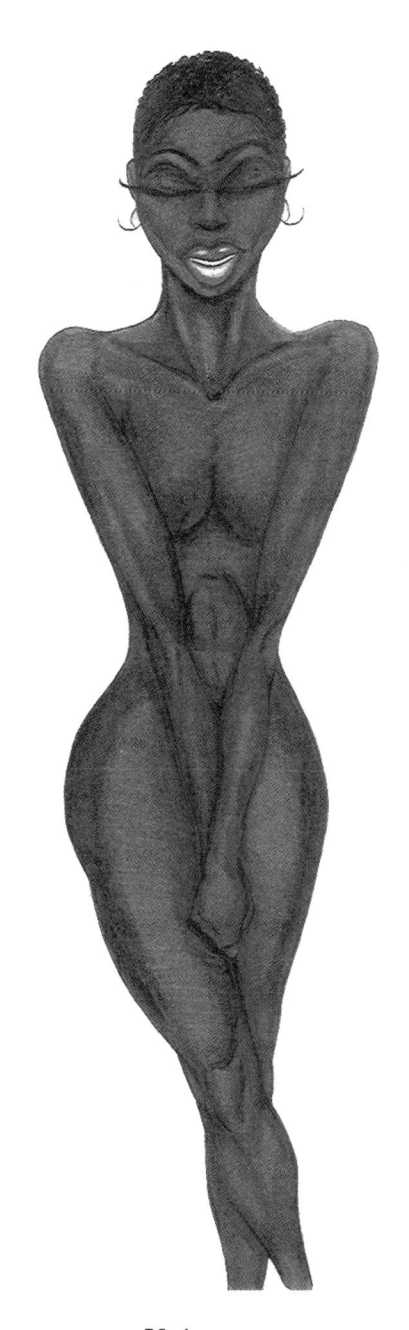

*Unique*

## How Black Mothers Are Setting Their Daughters up for Bad Relationships

You know, it's true that the "acorn doesn't fall far from the tree." The way your mate thinks, or any attitude problems she might have, usually arise from her mother's influence on her. In fact, in a recent survey done with African-American mothers around the world (ages 21–75), I discovered many African-American mothers are setting their daughters up from the beginning for bad relationships. Here are the reasons why:

1. If a man can't do anything for you, what good is he?

2. Marry a doctor or lawyer, or some other man with money.

3. Don't give your "stuff" away free!

4. A man's brain is between his legs.

5. A man should always have more than you.

6. You can find good loving anywhere, but only money pays the bills.

7. Never let your left hand know what your right hand is doing.

8. You can slap him, hit "him," but, *he better not lay a hand on you*.

9. A man is "supposed" to put all his money in one account. But, *you better always keep your something on the side*.

10. If you are poor or "broke," child, "your man don't love you." If he did, you wouldn't be "poor" or "broke."

11. No romance without finance.

12. As long as God keeps making black men, a "light-skinned woman" and a "big butt" will always be in demand.

13. If you are pretty and have a nice body, make a man pay to be with you or pay to be seen with you.

14. Black men don't know how to treat a woman.

15. White men treat black women better.

16. Don't choose a man too dark or too light. You don't want the kids coming out looking "blue" or "pale."

17. A good man is hard to find.

18. All black men are in jail.

19. Black men won't take care of their kids.

20. You don't have to work, girl. Just be a "lady in the street" and a "freak in the bedroom."

And the list goes on and on. Now, what is wrong with this picture is that it is "one-sided." African-American mothers are unconsciously and subliminally setting their daughters up for bad relationships. For example: If a man can't do anything for you, what good is he? A man should always have more than you. Don't give your "stuff" away free. Notice the words "you," "you," "you" keeps recurring. None of these examples say anything that even remotely addresses the issue of satisfying a man's needs.

Sex used to be the ultimate binding force in a relationship. But now, sex is being used as a weapon. "If you don't do this for me, then you don't get any." It seems men around the country agree.

According to *Cosmopolitan Magazine*, the words "selfish" and "unappreciative" are used by 70% of American husbands to describe their wives, and it is the number one thing that 75% of American husbands dislike about their mates.

Ask yourself, "Is the man of the '90s truly a dog, or just tired of being 'dogged?'"

In my personal study, I discovered that an average African-American man spends 75% of his life either chasing, trying to impress, or trying to make an African-American woman happy. On the other hand, an African-American woman spends 80% of her life trying to elevate herself or trying to make herself happy.

So, right now, let's see . . . can we "reprogram" ourselves? Let's put that advice Mama gave us on the "back burner" and explore and truly understand the needs, thinking, and sexuality of a being known as the black man.

## **Understanding a Black Man**

In order to truly appreciate and understand a black man, a woman must first learn what makes him "tick" and, in some cases, what makes him explode!

Over the past centuries, black men have experienced so much external pain and suffering that the last thing they need or want in a relationship is more of the same. For decades the black man has been at "war" with the legal system, the media, the job market, and society in general. And, I must admit, it has truly affected him in his relationships.

Before I tell you how to understand a black man, let me first tell you how a black man feels.

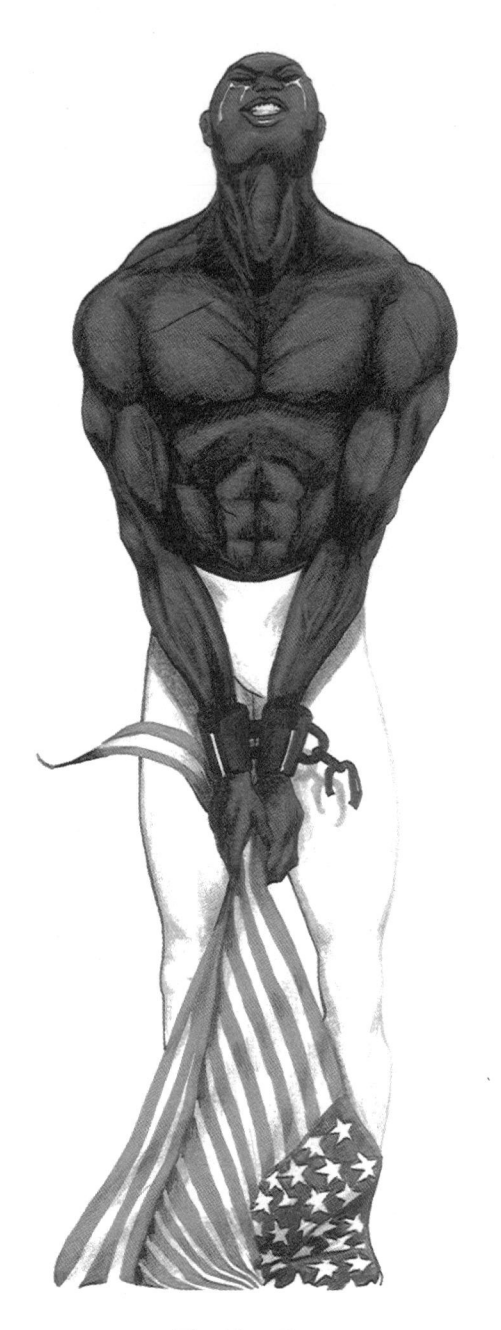

*The Flag Bearer*

## How Much Am I Worth as a Black Man?

I am supposed to be a role model for my kids, a father, and a provider for my family. How can I tell my family that I just lost my job? *How much would I be worth now as a black man?*

Rodney King, an African-American motorist, was caught on camera being beaten like a dog in the street. "We got them now!" he thought. "Well, Rodney, the blows really weren't connecting," they said. "You were actually in the wrong. According to the video and legal experts, *you were actually assaulting the police baton with your head.* The trial will prove what we say is true." "Trial? What trial? Am I always in the wrong, *even when the evidence proves that I am right*? I mean, as Rodney King, am I just another 'ordinary' black man?"

A single mother has a rough time making ends meet. I want to change all of that, so I approach her with kind words and a big smile. She then looks at me, swirls her head, and says, "Men aren't sh-t!" *Is this, too, what I'm worth as a black man?*

I cracked the books, and now I have a Ph.D., J.D., M.D., D.D.S., or C.P.A degree. I now live in a "posh" neighborhood. Nobody can get in or out without my permission. *But how much am I worth as "Frank Smith"—* just an ordinary, uneducated black man? Time after time, I know I've been more qualified for a job than the black woman. Yet she gets the promotion, mainly because she satisfies two governmental requirements: she is a female and she is black.

But that's not all. I secretly overhear "the brass" in the bathroom saying, "Keep giving the black women the job—pretty soon, they too will have a problem with the black man."

A prowler is seen in my ritzy neighborhood. I'm out jogging and the police stop me. I then put my hand in my pocket to pull out my medical doctor identification card. The policeman's partner shouts, "He's pulling out a gun!" Bang! Bang!

Am I always thought to be a "criminal" mainly due to the fact that I'm a black man?

I'm a young black man coming home from a party. A policeman stops me and says, "Hey, boy, get in the car! You can add to our collection. We already have over 800,000 of you in our system, quiet as that fact is kept. We have more of you in prison than in college! *Back to the station, Charlie, with another black man!*"

An ambulance is heading to my neighborhood. Another black man is killed mysteriously. "Label it drug-related," the detective says. *"It's only Tyrone. Just another black man."*

In the Million Man March, one million African-American men made a promise to the world that they would change. When will the African-American women do the same? *Or is it that we are the only ones with the "problem?" I mean the black men?*

How much am I worth as a black man is a question that millions of African-American men ask themselves every day. Because of his sensitive nature, and the *myth black women believe about him*, a black man will sometimes run away from his commitment, withdraw into himself, or lie, rather than communicating his true feelings.

## Myths Black Men Believe about Black Women

1. As long as you have finance, you will have romance.

2. Black women use sex as a weapon or as a reward.

3. Never let a black woman know how you truly feel.

4. Never let her know how much money you have.

5. Never let her know she's the "Fourth of July" in bed.

6. Never let her know she's attractive or "fine."

7. Never let her have too much power.

8. Never introduce her to your friends (she will either start confusion or sleep with one of them).

9. If she can't be happy, then neither will you.

10. Never get a black woman who is smarter than you.

11. Never be dependent on her or let her know you need her.

12. If it's "her" house and "her" car, she will throw it up in your face during an argument.

13. Always keep a "spare woman" on the side.

14. Never fall for her tears because she can lie and will lie with the best of them.

15. You can treat her well, give her the world, and she will still sleep with someone who does nothing for her.

16. You can't take a sister from the "projects" and make a "princess" out of her.

17. Black women love "roughnecks," or men who are dogs.

18. Never believe you are the only one she's sleeping with.

19. The only black woman you can truly trust is your mother.

20. A fair-skinned black woman is the worst kind of all. She thinks she's superior and "deserves the world."

21. If you don't want any strife in your life, never make a black woman your wife.

22. A black woman wants to burden you with her problems, but the moment you do the same, she loses interest or calls you a "wimp."

23. You have to "break her down" emotionally to keep her in check.

24. Never let a black woman get too close to your family. She will eventually try to turn them against you, too.

25. Keep her "barefoot, broke, and pregnant"... then you are "guaranteed" to stay in charge.

. . . and the list goes on and on.

In order to get a black man to open up and overcome the myths he's heard or believes about black women, a black woman must show him daily that she is not the monster she has been made out to be.

Now that you understand the feelings of a black man, let's further explore what a black woman can do further to "reprogram" her mate back into a trusting and loving being.

As you know, men in general have large and fragile egos. And you can certainly put black men in that category, too! While black men are the strongest men on earth, they are also the most sensitive. Now, how can you be both strong and sensitive? Well, it's quite simple. Look at the image of a black man in America:

"What good is he? I don't need anybody to bring me down. If you can't do anything for me, I don't want to be bothered."

Now, with so much hurt and anger inside of a black man, three needs have been created that supersede any other needs: (1) A need for *respect*; (2) *admiration*; and (3) *appreciation*. If a black woman can understand and fulfill these needs, then the "uncommitting dog" that society has labeled him to be will soon be ready to put on a leash. And he will view her as an asset instead of his adversary. Once that happens, that man who so frequently has "run away" from her will now run *towards* her.

*A Tribute to the Black Woman*

## Appreciating a Black Man and Woman

No other person has been more "misunderstood," "abused," and unappreciated than the black woman. Since her arrival in this country some 400 years ago, her "Afro-centric features" have been a target of mockery and ridicule. Now, what was once mockery and laughter have quickly turned into, "Doctor, I must get some of those" to "Hey, can you hook a girl up?" Those same full lips, big breasts, and round derrieres have now become a thing of beauty. And you cannot pick up a fashion or beauty magazine without seeing super models "flaunting" these attributes with pride.

To understand a black woman is also not difficult to do. Just as her male counterpart has special needs, so does she. Although black women share many needs with other women (see page 135), she too has three special needs that must also be met in order for her to remain "faithful" and "on a leash."

> 1. *Emotional Security*—Emotional security is defined as a feeling of assurance, devotion, or confidence. With so many women available to every black man, a woman wants to feel that her love is not "wasted." To a woman, her heart, mind, and body are a package deal. And, it is almost impossible to separate the three. Sometimes it is difficult for men to understand that *sex is an "emotional thing" to a woman first, then it becomes physical.* Too often, men take sex for granted. Sex has now become something to do when there isn't anything on HBO. To a woman, giving herself is the ultimate gift she can offer a man. And when her body and emotions are not appreciated, she too will withdraw into herself, or run to someone else. When everything else fails, she will sometimes resort to doing "wild and crazy" things.
>
> 2. *Financial Security*—Now, this is a word you hear quite often in the '90s. In fact, there have been many songs to re-

emphasize this point: "No Romance without Finance," "What Have You Done for Me Lately," and "Ain't Nothing Going On But the Rent." Very few African-American women grew up in households where there was cash readily available for their whims and wishes. Moreover, too many African-Americans grew up in single-parent households, watching their mothers struggle for every cent they got. And if a father was present, he often would use his "bread-winning" abilities as a mechanism to "control" his spouse. Because of so much emotional and physical abuse that a black woman experienced, women of the '90s have come to feel that "true" liberation began first by taking control of their own finances, then their romances. If a woman has her own "gold," she then feels that she can freely make, or assist in the making of, the "rules."

A secure woman of the '90s is not necessarily looking for a man who is Donald Trump. But every successful woman deserves a man with a "Donald Trump Starter Kit." What I mean by that is, she deserves a man who is striving to advance in his career and striving to reach a higher financial goal. This includes spending, saving, and investing wisely.

3. *Intimacy*—The word "intimacy" has puzzled men for years. Too many men believe that intimacy is defined as the ability to "throw that thing." But this is only a small fraction of its true meaning. Intimacy first began with attending to a woman's emotional needs first, then her physical needs. Intimacy is lying in bed, caressing your mate, holding her, comforting her, reinforcing to her that her true beauty is not necessarily an outward attribute, but an inward one as well. Intimacy is picking up the telephone and saying, "I just called to say 'I love you.'"

Intimacy is noticing a new dress, the smell of her perfume, or her new hairstyle. Intimacy is driving across town at 3:00 in the morning in the cold just to bring her some chicken soup. Intimacy is catching a cold yourself because you were "dumb" enough to be caught out at 3:00 a.m. in the cold!

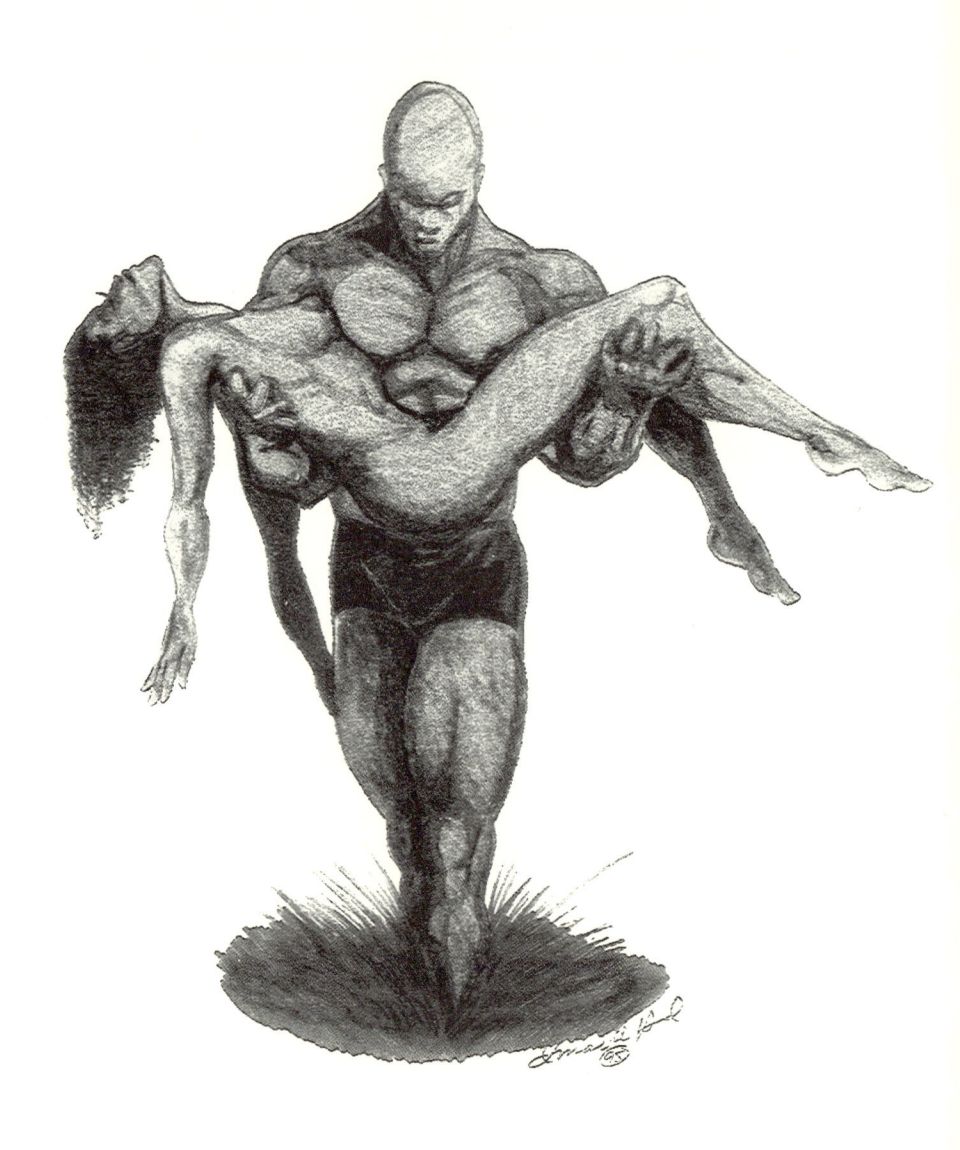

*My "Protector" or My "Abuser"*

## Transforming an "Abused" Black Woman Back into a Loving Being

According to Planned Parenthood, 67% of black households are headed by black women. African-Americans have the lowest commitment rate and the highest divorce rate of all minorities (Orientals, Asians, Jews, Latinos, etc.).

A black woman is 70% more likely to "brutalized" by her spouse and 52% likely to be unmarried past the age of 35. With so much abuse and uncertainty a black woman faces, all she truly wants in a black man is *"someone upon whom she can depend, someone who will protect her and someone she doesn't have to worry about being protected from."*

In order to break down the defenses of an abused woman, it will take time and a lot of patience. It is a slow process. But to start the process of returning her to being a loving and trusting woman, one must first begin with honesty and appreciation.

Now, because of centuries of abuse, centuries of black mothers telling their daughters never to be dependent upon a black man, and centuries of being forced to adapt, improvise, and overcome, these negative reinforcements have produced a modern-day black woman who is strong and independent. Men sometimes interpret this strength as the woman "trying to wear the pants." But this is the farthest thing from the truth. In the '90s, both spouses wear the pants. But black women would gladly wear the dress if they could get the "real men" to stand up.

## We Both Wear the Pants . . .
## But Will the Real Men Please Stand up?

How often have you heard a male say, "I'm the man of the house," "That's a man's responsibility," "I make the money," "I take care of the family," "I fix the car," or "I make the decisions"? Well, today, the women are making just as much—or more—money as their male counterparts. Many are head of single-parent homes. They take care of the family, make the bread, bring it home, slice it, serve it, wash the dishes after it, then go outside and shoot "hoops" or play football with the boys, teach the daughter self-defense, wash the car, change the tire, catch a Bulls game on TV, drink a cold one, help the kids with their homework, and tell them about the "birds and the bees." Then, they tuck the kids in and check the windows and doors to make sure that all is safe. Does doing all these things make the woman a man, too? In the '90s, both spouses wear the pants, but how do we get the "real" men to please stand up?

As we know, physically abusing a woman, sexual intimacies, and fathering kids does not make a man. Nor does having a harem of women on the side. A real man is defined as the male of the human species who takes care of his kids because he wants to and not because he's made to. He respects his wife, treats her like a queen, and values her opinion. He is never too busy for his kids and is devoted to his family. He makes the money and brings it home to his family and does not stray. He cooks the meal, serves it, and washes the dishes afterwards. He's strong, yet weak and not afraid to cry. He is there when you need him, and you always know where to reach him. He's a friend, a buddy, and at peace with his Maker. Both spouses may "wear the pants," but a woman just wants the "real men" to please stand up!

*I Am There For You*

## Why the Available Black Men Are Excluding Black Women As "Ideal Mates"

I must admit, the Million Man March was a landmark event, and a much needed event in waking up African-American men everywhere. But in order to keep African-American men true to their word, and to keep the African-American family strong, African women must come off the "we are the only injured party" list, the "we are the perfect angels" list, and accept part of the blame.

In the three years it took me to complete this book, I interviewed thousands of available, educated, successful African-American men as well as servicemen, and they openly admitted that relationships between the African-American man and the African-American woman have not just gotten bad, but *critical*. Moreover, many of these same African-American men are contemplating writing all black women off completely and feel as though the grass may be greener on the other side.

In recent studies done by numerous magazines and publications around the county (*Ebony* magazine, *Jet*, *Essence*, *Parade* magazine, *USA Today*, etc.), it was discussed that interracial dating in the '90s has reached an all-time high.

In fact, *Parade* magazine did a national survey among African-American men and women and discovered that 85% of the men had dated interracially compared to about 65% of the African-American women. Now, this is America, and you are certainly free to "do your own thing." After all, the essence of any relationship is love, not *color*. But get this: out of the 85% of the African-American men who had dated inter-racially, 65% of these same men said, and I quote, "*We are daily seeking and hoping to find any nationality of women to marry other than black women.*" Now, that's pretty sad, especially considering that about 75% of the African-American women said, "*They will gladly stick with and support their black men.*"

In fact, the top 100 black "money makers" and well-to-do African-American men are *married to or involved with* every nationality of women except African-American women:

# African-American Relationships 185

1. Tiger Woods (first Asian-African-American to win the Masters Golf Tournament)—Caucasian.

2. Donovan Bailey (Canadian Gold Medalist and the "Fastest Man in the World")—Caucasian.

3. Lord John Taylor of Warwick (the only African-American to become a member of England's House of Lords)—Caucasian.

4. Meadowlark Lemon (founder of the Harlem Globetrotters basketball team)—Caucasian.

5. Barry Bond (baseball player)—Caucasian.

6. Arsenio Hall (talk show host)—Caucasian, Latino, Asian.

7. Billy Dee Williams (actor and movie idol)—Oriental, Caucasian.

8. Quincy Jones (producer)—European.

9. Michael Jackson (entertainer)—Caucasian.

10. Richard Roundtree (actor)—Caucasian.

11. James Brown (entertainer)—Caucasian.

12. Al Jarreau (singer)—Caucasian.

13. Sidney Poitier (actor)—Caucasian.

14. Wesley Snipes (actor)—Asian.

15. James Earl Jones (actor)—Caucasian.

16. Gregory Hines (actor)—Caucasian.

17. Charles Barkley (basketball player)—Caucasian.

18. Reginald Lewis (former CEO of Beatrice Foods)—Asian.

19. Herschel Walker (football player)—Italian.

20. Pelé (soccer player)—Caucasian/Latino/Portuguese.

21. Clarence Thomas (Supreme Court Justice)—Caucasian.

22. Montel Williams (talk show host)—Caucasian.

23. Robert Parish (basketball player)—Arab.

24. Lonnie Bristow (first African-American to head the American Medical Association)—Caucasian.

25. Frank Bruno (boxer)—Caucasian.

26. Kevin Johnson (basketball player)—Caucasian.

27. Lionel Richie (entertainer)—Caucasian.

28. Dennis Rodman (basketball player)—Caucasian.

29. The Artist formerly known as "Prince" (entertainer)—Latino.

30. Marcus Allen (football player)—Caucasian.

31. Al Cowling (O. J. Simpson's best friend and ex-football player)—Caucasian.

32. J. D. Nicholas (singer with The Commodores)—Filipino.

33. Fred Williamson (actor, producer)—Caucasian.

34. Ernie Hudson (actor)—Caucasian.

35. George Stanford Brown (actor)—Caucasian.

36. Berry Gordy (founder of Motown Records)—Caucasian.

37. Ben Vereen (actor)—Caucasian.

38. Eriq Lasalle (star of TV series "ER")—Caucasian.

39. Cuba Gooding, Jr. (star of the movie "Jerry McGuire" and "Boyz in the Hood")—Caucasian.

40. Yaphet Kotto (actor)—Filipino.

41. Kirby Pluckett (baseball player)—Latino.

42. Thomas Mikal Ford (costar of the TV show "Martin")—Jamaican.

43. Leon Isaac Kennedy (actor/producer)—Filipino.

44. Harry Belafonte (actor)—Caucasian.

45. Darren Harewood (actor—"The Jesse Owen Story")—Caucasian.

46. Ben Johnson (Canadian Gold Medalist)—Caucasian.

47. Glenn Rice (basketball player)—Latino.

48. Wynton Marsalis (musician)—Caucasian.

49. Clarence Gilyard (actor, star of "Walker, Texas Ranger")—Caucasian.

50. Gary Payton (basketball player)—Caucasian.

And the list goes on and on. You know, there's a saying that "water seeks its own level." But when it comes to the rich, educated, successful African-American men as well as servicemen, it seems these sought-after men are "passing over" and "dissing" (disrespecting) educated, high-powered, and wealthy African-American women just for "plain Jane" women of other nationalities. The big question is, *Why?*

1. The #1 complaint that available African-American men, as well as servicemen, have with the African-American women of the '90s is that when it comes to relationships, "African-American women are extremely selfish. It's all about *their needs, their wants, their desires, their happiness*, and that they don't care about anyone else.

2. African-American women of the '90s are "extremely materialistic." It's always a game of "Let's Make A Deal" ... You do this for me, I'll do this for you. According to these same men, white girls and women of other races and nationalities are "gold diggers," too, but the biggest difference is that women of other nationalities know how to hide it. It's not as obvious. You can see a sister coming a mile away. Black women will scan you from head to toe, and if your shoes are not of a designer brand, they will quickly turn up their noses and put you on their "he can't do anything for me" list. *White girls and women of other nationalities cater to black men's egos.* Let's face it: we all like to have someone tell us how wonderful we are. You can always catch more flies with honey than with vinegar. Black women want to be put on a pedestal and be complimented, but they don't want to do the same. They often tell each other, "Never let a man know that he looks good and, whatever you do, never let a man know that you are checking him out." On the other hand, white girls will walk up to you and tell the "brother" that he's all of that and a "twinkie" on the side. For example, if a brother has a nice car, a black woman would check him out "slyly" out of the corner of her eye, while a white girl would flag him down and probably want to jump in the car with him.

3. With black women, if you don't have as much as she has, or if your credentials are less impressive, she will look down on you and once again put you on her "he can't do anything for me" list.

4. Black women have too many "hangups" about men and past relationships. For example, a man is always supposed to "foot the bill." He is supposed to do this for her: 55% of the married men I interviewed also "exhaled" on their

wives and black women in general: "Black women want you to spend *your money on her* and she always wants to spend *her* money on her. Now, who spends money on the black man? Who cares? It's not about him in the first place!"

5. According to 90% of the black men interviewed, black women to them have as their definition of a good man "a BMW, Mercedes-driving, Hugo Boss suit-wearing, briefcase-carrying, 'I'll do anything for you' man in the shade of black."

6. If you ever want a relationship to get shaky or a black woman to disrespect you, go broke or be put in a situation in which she will have to take care of you and help you out.

7. Black women's personalities are entirely too *dominant*. Many of them can't turn it off, tone it down, relax, and just be a woman. You are always emotionally fighting with them; moreover, when arguing, they will always want to have the last word. On the other hand, according to these same African-American men with white girlfriends, during an argument, their European counterpart will express the problem quietly, rationally and always ask, "Baby, is it me? Am I the one to blame?" The same men said that with their black girlfriends or wives, the argument was always his "fault," and the problem was always a result of something he didn't do "to" her or "for" her.

8. Eighty-eight percent of the black men said that black women had an inherent "mean streak" in them. For example, a professional athlete for the Dallas Cowboys,

whom I'll call "Charlie," revealed that with his black girlfriend, he could walk into the house on top of the world, and she could be angry. With his being happy and her being angry, it made her even angrier. What she would do then is to say or do something that she knew would bring him down or cause an argument. Once she was successful in making him angry, or in "bursting his bubble," she could then smile with happiness. What makes this scenario even more of a concern is that 90% of the men said they have experienced the same thing! If a black woman can't be happy, or can't be the center of attention, then nobody will.

9. Black women will become enraged if you assist someone other than her financially.

10. Black women are very vindictive. Payback is a bitch! What is more astounding is that only 5% of the black men I interviewed desired a white woman for the mystique or saw them as a "forbidden fruit."

11. When it comes to lovemaking, women of other races set no boundaries. With black women, once they are satisfied from doing the "wild thing," or the "nasty," then it's a matter of "Hey, I'm sorry for you."

12. Their mothers "program" them to be selfish. For example, if a man doesn't have anything, what good is he? You don't need any help to starve to death. You can do badly all by yourself.

13. Black women are extremely stubborn. By the time you "break down" their defenses, you will either be "burned out" or you shall have lost interest.

14. Black women are always trying to impress their friends and are extremely status conscious. As long as you can make her look good, then it's all good. But if your status or financial position changes, then it's on to the next person. In fact, one noted physician "exhaled" on his wife. "I noticed when my wife went to her class reunion, she always introduced me not as Terry Williams, her husband, but as Doctor Terry Williams—'a heart surgeon.' At home, she always tells me she is not impressed by my being a surgeon. I wonder what made her change her mind?"

15. A black woman wants to live a "soap opera" life. This is reality. I am not Victor Newman, she is not "Nikki," and this is not "The Young and the Restless!"

On the other hand, what's good for the goose is also good for the gander. Here are some of the reasons that 65% of the African-American women revealed as causing them to cross the color line:

1. Black men don't know how to treat black women. According to them, how to treat a woman involves: respecting her opinion, her desires, and not just seeing her only as a sex object, but as a person who wants "emotional" love as well as physical love.

2. Black men are physically abusive to women. Instead of talking about a problem, they hit.

3. Black men look for a "sister" who has it going on, then sponge off her. Seventy percent of the women revealed that they don't mind helping the man who has less, as long as he's trying.

4. Some black men are not ambitious enough.

5. White men can open doors that black men can't.

6. The good black men are married or chasing white girls.

7. Black women cite lack of availability of compatibility in black men. For example, they cite discrepancies in income, status, etc.

8. White men are more open-minded, like to travel, or experiment.

9. Black women have been emotionally hurt or abused in their black relationships.

10. White men "pamper" their women and want to make them happy.

You know, there are "three sides" to every story, not two. Those three sides are: a man's side; a woman's side; and the "truth."

In hopes of arriving at the truth so that African-Americans can once and for all put this age-old problem to rest, I decided to personally conduct a three-year in-depth study just to trace the root of this growing problem. Before going into the reasons behind this growing phenomenon, let me first reveal the findings of my study. My study also revealed that 65% of the rich, available, successful, educated African-American men as well as servicemen are truly married or involved with non-African-American women.

In addition, my study revealed that white women alone have "swooped up" 52% of the African-American medical doctors, 48% of the African-American lawyers, 50% of the African-American CEOs, and 60% of the African-American millionaires.

While successful African-American women are complaining about the shortage of "good" and available black men, non-African-American women around the country are saying that they don't know why African-American women are having such a difficult time because "they" don't have a problem in finding themselves good black men.

This survey also points out that African-American women had first crack at 92% of the African-American men who are now rich, powerful, and successful, but kicked them to the curb too soon.

It was also discovered that while non-African-American women are marrying the top of the line African-American men, it seems African-American men are settling for "plain Jane" women of other races.

Additionally, it was found that based on what non-African-American women teach their daughters about getting and keeping a man, *in the '90s non-African-American women* are 75% more likely to "hook" an African-American millionaire.

Lastly, it was discovered that black millionaires seldom ask for a prenuptial agreement once they marry non-African-American women. In fact, after 1965, 58% of the African-American millionaires whose mates were African-American women required a prenuptial agreement as a prerequisite to marriage. Only 5% of the African-American millionaires whose wives are white are protected by a prenuptial agreement. And what is even more astounding than that is, not even one half of one percent of the African-American millionaires whose mates are Asian, Oriental, Latino, Jewish, Italian, Arabic, or Philippine women are protected by a prenuptial agreement.

It seems in the '90s, once African-American men marry non-African-American women, their careers soar, and they very seldom return to African-American women.

Now let's explore the reasons behind this growing problem. My study revealed that there were four reasons that so many African men and women in the '90s were finding it difficult in making a "love connection," and once they made a "love connection," they found it difficult in staying happy and committed.

Reason #1 is the growing number of African-American mothers who are unconsciously setting their daughters up for bad relationships.

Reason #2: African-American men themselves. Far too many men believe and practice the theory I call the "K-9 Theory": An abundant supply of women, minus a shortage of black men, equals a DOG . . . Cujo, Lassie, Rin-Tin-Tin, Snoopy, and Scooby-Doo. Now, if I subtract the black men who are in prison and add them to the number of black men who are "hooked on drugs" or homosexual and then multiply that times the number of black women who don't have a man, the answer will always equal "more women for me!"

Reason #3 is society. Too many African-American women are letting television and western standards dictate what happiness is, as well as defining for them what a "good" man is. For example, he must drive a certain kind of car, make a certain income, have a certain job title, a particular kind of home, etc.

Reason #4 is . . . authors who are supposed to be experts on relationships! Far too many writers are jumping on the bandwagon and cashing in on the "malebashing!" I realize that authors must make a living, but whatever happened to responsibility and helpfulness?

Now, why is it that 65% of the rich, successful, available, and educated African-American men marry non-African-American women? Shouldn't a black man want to keep the money, education, success, and power in his own race? Shouldn't a black man care about the future and strength of the black nation? Shouldn't a black woman be more qualified to satisfy his needs? Shouldn't a black man also feel that since African-American women have been denied the stability, admiration, and luxury in life that he has a "duty" to consider here, if for no other reason than the general principle?

In order to answer these questions honestly, we must first explore a few things: #1, the needs of a black man; #2, what the *African-American mother* is teaching her daughter; and #3, what non-African-American mothers teach their daughters about getting and keeping a man.

Let's explore #1, the needs of a black man. As I mentioned earlier, a black man has three needs: *respect, admiration,* and *appreciation.* Because there is so much pressure and stress that African-American men have to face on a daily basis, I must add two more needs to this list: *emotional support* and *peace of mind.* These five needs are not only important in getting a black man to marry within his race, but important in getting him to fall in love, getting him to the altar, important in getting a 50-year warranty with your marriage, and important in keeping him trained, "whipped," faithful, and on a leash. The woman who can satisfy these needs will never have to worry about her man leaving her, cheating on her, or kicking her to the curb, regardless of how much younger, prettier, finer, smarter, or richer the competition may be. You would think with the shortage of available black men that African-American women would be standing in line to fill this order. But to my surprise, this was the furthest thing from the truth. While non-African-American women satisfy their men's five basic needs on a daily basis, 93% of these available African-American men have never experienced their mate's asking what she can do to make him happy. Ninety-six percent of these available men had never experienced their mate's ever saying, "I appreciate you"; and 86% of these men had never had their mates apologize during an argument. On the other hand, what 73% of these same men have experienced is their mate's saying things so "ugly" to them that they broke down and cried. It seems in the '90s, the strong and supportive black women that black men have praised for centuries have been unconsciously "reprogrammed" by their mothers to be "masters of the game" in *materialism, manipulation,* and *deception.* They've been taught how not to get and keep a man, how to sabotage your marriage, and how to turn a strong and caring black man against his friends, his family, and against all black women forever.

Having talked to African-American mothers around the country, from ages 21–75, I found that these are the tools that far too many of them are giving their daughters with which to build a happy, trusting, and lasting relationship:

1. Never put all your eggs in one basket (yet African-American women want a man's undying devotion).

2. If a man can't do anything for you, what good is he? What about how *she* can enhance *him*?

3. Ain't nothing going on but the rent. She knew the rent was going on before she moved into that expensive "pad."

4. I can't stand no whining men—I am not your mother! Yet she wants to be cuddled, supported until her problem is solved.

5. If he can't give you what you want, somebody else will. Yet men who think like that are considered dogs!

6. All black men want to do is "lay up" and use you. Yet black women use sex to manipulate and control a black man.

7. Cook a meal! I work just like you! What time are you taking *me* out? I also discovered that many African-American women of the '90s can't cook and even consider it beneath them to do so!

8. Child, don't give your "stuff" away free! Too many African-American women believe that once she sleeps

with a man, he should pay her bills and provide anything else her mind craves.

9. Don't believe anything he tells you. Check it out first! Yet, she wants to be trusted and even wants her spouse to defend her and take her side when both of you know she's wrong.

10. Never let a man know he looks good because he'll think every woman wants him. As long as he feels that you are the best he can do, he'll always be in "check." On the other hand, African-American women crave attention and love to be complimented, and many of them will even go into debt to be the best-dressed woman in the office.

And the list goes on and on, reinforcing the point that many African-American mothers are unconsciously setting their daughters up for bad relationships.

As I have mentioned, white women alone have managed to "swoop up" 52% of the African-American medical doctors, 48% of the African-American attorneys, 50% of African-American CEOs, and 60% of the African-American millionaires.

Now, the reason that white women are so successful in getting the richest and the most successful African-American men is in the way their mothers "programmed" and prepared them for relationships. Here are a few things they are taught:

1. Give a man respect and he'll respect you.

2. Stand by your man.

3. Always think long-term.

4. You can't judge a book by its cover.

5. Always go for the best.

6. Marry a man who is rich or has the potential to be rich.

7. You can catch more flies with honey than with vinegar.

8. A smile and a good attitude will carry you a long way.

The study also revealed that African-American women had first crack at 92% of these rich and successful men, but they kicked them to the curb too soon. You see, 98% of the black men who are now rich and successful started with nothing but a "dream," "ambition," and a vision.

In fact, when I talked to 100 of the richest and most powerful men whose mates are non-African-American women, what they remembered most about their struggle to the top was the number of insults and emotional abuse they experienced at the hands of African-American women. For example, "You can't do anything for me. Please call me when you get it together" or "You want to be a doctor? Ha ha! You need to get a job and get your mother out of the projects first!" But, strange as it may seem, as soon as these men become doctors, lawyers, businessmen, entertainers, CEOs, and millionaires, these same black women who once turned their noses up at them are now beating down their doors pursuing them. Once he turns to a woman of another race, he is then labeled as a "dog" or a sell-out.

What African-American women fail to realize is that if a woman can't be with a man when he's down, most men will not allow her to be with him when he's up. In fact, another sad thing this study revealed was that after 1965, 58% of the 100 richest African-American men whose mates were African-American women required a prenuptial agreement as a prerequisite to marriage. But only 5% of the African-American millionaires whose mates were white are protected by a prenuptial agreement and not even one half of one percent of African-American man whose mates are Asian, Oriental, Latino, Jewish, Italian, Arabic or Philippine women are protected by a prenuptial agreement.

The sad thing about a prenuptial agreement is, of course, that it is telling the woman, "I love you, but I don't trust you. And I feel that this marriage is not going to last. I feel the main reason you married me is because of what I have or who I am. So, to feel comfortable in marrying you, I must now protect myself as well as my assets against you."

The reason so many successful and available African-American men would gladly pass over single and educated African-American women for "plain Jane" women of other races is because there is "respect, admiration, appreciation, emotional support, and peace of mind." Such a "hierarchy" of needs in his happiness results in the man being instantly drawn to any woman who can satisfy them, regardless of her race or status. And she will keep him on a leash, even when the black woman cannot.

Therefore, always keep in mind, a black man will marry down in order to be happy while a black woman will marry up and "think" she will be happy!

I also noticed in this three-year study that once African-American men marry non-African-American women, it seems their careers soar. The reason behind that is that even the strongest man needs emotional support. A man cannot prosper if he's constantly fighting or running up behind a woman. Earlier, I mentioned that an average African-American man spends 75% of his life chasing, trying to impress or trying to make an African-American woman happy, while the average American woman spends 80% of her life trying to elevate herself or trying to make "herself" happy.

It's sad that so many African-American women miss out on so many good African-American men because it seems they want them only when they become successful. But during the time of "uncertainty" or "trouble," so many don't stick around long enough to see how the story might end. An African-American woman should always keep in mind that "the cream always rises to the top," and tough times don't last, but tough people do. I also discovered that in the '90s, the strong black women that you've heard about so frequently are usually African-American men's mothers—and very seldom their mates.

The last thing this three-year study revealed is that once black men marry non-African-American women, they seldom go back to African-American women. The reason for this is that an African-American man will "date" a non-African-American woman out of curiosity, but he will marry her out of love and frustration. Even when I talk to some of the powerful, richest, and most sought after African-American men in the country, 95% of them said that *"an African-American woman was always the first choice."* They also realize that all African-American women are not alike. But because they have been "dogged out," let down, emotionally abused, or left hanging so frequently, now the innocent African-American women have to suffer with the guilty. And now, when it comes to "turning back" to or "committing" to an African-American woman in a monogamous relationship, they desperately want to do so, but many of them are just shell-shocked.

They also realize that the African-American community and so many African-American women feel they are "sell-outs," but it was the African-American woman who sold them out. And so many of them seem to "sell you out" when you need them the most.

I find it very sad to discover that for decades so many African-American mothers have taught their daughters that you can do bad all by yourself. Now, decades later, so many of their daughters are "doing well" and they continue to be by themselves. So, until the modern-day African-American women look within themselves and realize they, too, must share the blame for the failure of so many African-American relationships, and if a black woman is to truly keep her man on a "leash," she must be willing to give as much as she is expecting to receive. Conversely, if the black man is to rise, prosper, and be totally happy, the black woman cannot and will not always be the focus of his universe. If she needs to be, she will forever be searching for a soul mate, forever be a divorce statistic, forever feel the shortage of available black men, and most of all, forever be excluded as an ideal mate.

By no means interpret this chapter as "African-American Woman Bashing!" You see, when a man loves a woman, he will tell her to her face what people are saying behind her back. When a man loves a woman, he will run "toward" her when there's trouble and not "away" from her.

After doing this three-year in-depth study, I'll even admit, some black men truly are dogs! But the majority of the sought after rich, successful, available African-American men as well as servicemen are so tired of being "dogged."

## Conclusion
## The Truth Shall Set You Free

In order for your mate to change or improve, you must first communicate all hidden feelings and hang-ups you have about them. Remember, your mate can't fix it unless they first know it's broken.

In fact, I'll end this chapter as well as this book, with a letter that expresses the honest feelings and hang-ups that seem to be sending so many rich, available, educated and successful African-American men to every nationality of women except African-American women.

**My Beautiful Black Woman, There's Something You Should Know...**

I'm at a difficult time in my life... a time that many African-American men had to face before me... a time in which there is chaos and confusion at home, confusion at work, confusion in society, and confusion in the black community. I feel pressure coming in from all sides, and no one to turn to. I want to leave! I want to run! I want to get away. I want to be understood. I feel that for years, everyone, including you, my black woman, has chiseled at my "base," hoping I would fall. I am so tired of arguing and fighting. I'm looking out the window of our $250,000 house on the lake, with "his and hers" sport Lexus automobiles in the driveway. I'm looking at two beautiful kids coming home from the best private school money can buy. I'm looking at Chippendale furniture, "plaques of achievement" on the wall, and a scrapbook of our wedding day, and the promises and dreams that we both shared. I'm looking at a closet full of designer clothes. Oh, by the way, the mayor invited us to his masquerade ball. I know that will make you happy. You have finally "arrived." You are now a "socialite" and on everybody's "A list." I'm looking at our wedding pictures on the dresser, and as I write this letter, tears fill my eyes and sadness fills my heart. I am not only crying for what I am contemplating doing, but the reason behind it. Put the telephone down, you don't have to call 9-1-1. I'm not thinking about putting a gun to my head and end it all, but what I *am* about to do and the reasons behind it could be just as destructive. Not only will you and I and the kids feel the pain, but so will our ancestors and the generations to come. I'm sure by now you are aware that the closeness we once shared is no longer there. I'm sleeping in silk pajamas, on silk sheets, next to a stranger. Let's not kid ourselves. You and I both know that the only thing we have in common now are the children.

To this day, I still feel the only reason that you were attracted to me was because I had a title, and I could give you the lifestyle, the status, and all the material things your mother never had. It seems the more we have, the more you want. And when I mention the word "love," it's a big joke. To me, it seems you are always trying to impress your friends. And frankly, I can't stand any of those "dizzy snobs from the projects." An evening with them is always, "Girl, my man promised to take me to Paris" or "Girl, that's nothing, we are going to buy a villa in the South of France" or "Why would you buy a villa in France when all the 'right people' are buying property in Rio?"

It seems you have forgotten how to be a woman. You want to wear the dress and the pants. The tower of strength and independence that once attracted me to you and made you a prize "catch" have now turned out to be, "I don't need a man for anything." We are constantly at war with each other, trying to get and keep the upper hand. And it frightens me, because now society and the law have given it to you, and you often use it against me. I now feel that you no longer need me. You make twice as much money as I do and when we are arguing, you never fail to let me know it.

The world embraces you, while it ridicules me. I remember before the "M.D." was added to my name, I overheard you telling one of your "wanna-be" friends that I was not on your level. It's funny that the "little" that I had I gladly shared with you. But during an argument, what was once *our house* has suddenly become *your house, your car, and your money!* It seems it's always a "no-win" situation with you. You are very argumentative; you have grown extremely selfish; you've forgotten how to relax and have fun! It seems you don't know who you really are. Society is dictating your life . . . what you should think . . . how you should look . . . and even what you should drive. You know for yourself the only reason you wanted that Lexus was because society said it was the car that successful blacks drove.

Last year it was the BMW, and next year, what car will it be then? It has gotten so bad, the love and affection I once had for you is gone. Now, when I kiss you in public, you are so worried about your "reputation," how you are dressed, who's looking at you, or what others may think. Right now, I couldn't give a damn about what anyone may think. I just want to be happy, to have "peace of mind." Regardless of how hard I try, there seems to be no peace with you. Dealing with you has caused my mind to be in turmoil, in doubt, in rage. My beautiful black woman, you have changed on me. I am so tired of you and the world telling me what I am not. Has it occurred to you that I have feelings? I pretend that I am "hard" and uncaring, but I have to protect my emotions and feelings. Has it ever occurred to you that you could get more out of me by telling me everything that I am, instead of always telling me what I am not? Has society turned you against me, too? Do you now see me as your enemy instead of your partner? Why do we compete against each other? We're fighting over crumbs, while the "real dogs" are getting all the meat! Let me ask you a little trivia question, since you love to play mind games (and I must admit, you are truly the "master of the game"): What is the difference between a black man and a black woman who is making $200,000? A black man who is making $200,000 per year would gladly share it with a black woman, but a black woman making $200,000 a year would look down on a black man who was making less and say, "I don't want him, he's not on my level."

I am so tired of the world blaming me for everything: crime, welfare, drugs . . . you put overtime in on your job, but you are on an hourly wage with me. I guess it's true: you get what you pay for. Maybe I should have put you on layaway and just come back when I could afford you. Whatever happened to the time when my word was law, my wishes and hopes and dreams were the way it should be? Now society tells you that my words mean nothing and that I am nothing.

Whatever happened to the time when you believed in me? When you cherished me and we worshipped the same God? When we had the same dreams and worked together, cried together, prayed together? Whatever I had was yours. We shared our wealth. Nobody could tell you what I wasn't because you knew first-hand who I was and what I was. There was no mistrust between us. There were no "pre-nuptial" lawyers, and your mother was in the "amen corner" keeping up "sh-t."

Whatever happened to the time when the little money we did have wasn't enough to put in the "First" National Bank, so we put it in the "Second" National Bank: your bra?! What happened to "trust me?" My beautiful black woman, you have changed on me. Remember the time when the only secret we had was the secret that I "kind of like you?" Remember when we made a promise that we would love each other forever? Remember the only restraint that I worried about was restraining myself from kissing you from head to toe? Remember when we argued, and the best part was making up? The best part of it all was to throw my arms around you and feel the texture of your braided or kinky hair and take my finger around the fullness of your lips and grab the softness of your "onion" body. Do you remember when we used to look at a falling star and make a wish? You always asked me what my wish was. Well, that wish was always the same wish I made on every falling star—that we would never be apart.

My beautiful African woman, you have changed on me. You are caught up chasing the "American Dream." It's funny, your "onion" body, your hips, legs, breasts, lips, eyes, and hair that made you stand out from other women, you've grown ashamed of it all, tried to hide it, lose it. You even wanted to change the color of your eyes because "they" said it was not "chic" or even "vogue." But I always defended you and told you over and over again that your "distinctive features" had always been, and will always be, in style. But of course, you always questioned "my word" and opinion. Not only were you dissatisfied with you... the more you achieved, and the higher you climbed, the more critical you became of me and the lower you put me down. You then compared me to my "counterpart." Instead of defending me, you offended me. Look, my beautiful black woman, I came to this country 400 years ago with nothing, and I think I have done damn good to get this far. I held you up while you put me down. I have worked my butt off to give you all that you thought you wanted. But what have you given in return? *Nothing but pain, misery, and grief.* I cannot be responsible for the hurt your father, ex-lover, or whoever inflicted upon you. I can be responsible only for the joy and happiness that I tried so desperately to have with you.

Now you ask me why I'm thinking about crossing the color line? Why would I want to tread in "shallow" and forbidden waters? For years I have been drowning with you. I have fought off sharks while you swam to safety and often left me hanging. You know, it's funny: whenever you have a problem, you have your girlfriend, psychiatrist, the law, and the courts to confide in. But where do I go? Who listens to, and honestly cares about, me? I can't cry on your shoulder because you will take my sensitivity and vulnerability and throw them up in my face.

What do I want from you? When I stumble, brush me off. Tell me what I am and not always what I am not. Embrace me, don't ridicule me. When I achieve, rejoice with me, and when I fall, lift me up instead of "crawling" over my back and betting the "spoils" from my demise. It's lonely at the top ... but I just want to be happy, even if it means being happy with another race at the bottom. So be it! As I have said before, I give up on you. I will try this one last time to hang in there with you. What I want from you is someone to talk to; I want you to call me at work just to say "I love you," "I miss you," or "I'm thinking about you." I want to feel that I'm the most important person in your life, and that you will give up everything, including your career, for me. Of course, I could never be that selfish, but I would love to think that you would.

My beautiful black woman, I'm writing this letter from the "prison of my soul." Sometimes I lie awake at night in my silk pajamas and look at the M.D., Ph.D., J.D., C.P.A. plaques, and ask myself, "Are degrees, money, and titles the only things that make me desirable to you?"

For years, society has told you that you deserve better. But right now, I am tired of fighting with society, the law, the job, and you. For 400 years, I've been getting my butt kicked by everyone. So, now I know I deserve better. For once in your life, listen to me, *listen to what I have to say*, let me have the last word, listen to what I want and what I need. This is my final attempt, and my final plea, to reach you. Maybe I just need some time, some space, some air, something new, something different. But what I do know, my beautiful black woman, is that the next time I see you, I want to see a change in you. I want to see a change in you that spring brings after a harsh winter. I want to see the supportive, strong., sensual, loving, kind-hearted, trusting black woman that I have relied on and grown to love. If I can't have her, and continue to have to deal with the cold, insensitive, selfish, materialistic, money-grubbing, trying-to-keep-up-with-the-Joneses woman that you have become, then you know where you can find 65% of the available black men, and 60% of the black men with money. And that place, my beautiful black woman, is at "Miss Ann's House."

Yours truly, Y.L.M.N.O.C. (You Leave Me No Other Choice)

P. S. Here is something else for you to think about: For years, I've been waiting to exhale on you. In 1995, the University of Chicago did a survey on the "Disappearance of the Black Man." They predicted by the year 2000, 70% of all black men will either be in jail, unemployed, dead, or strung out on drugs. Now tell me, where does that leave you and the black family?

I cannot and will not continue to deal with you "on my case," society on my back, and the weight of the world on my shoulders.

*No Relief*

# Note from the Author

Thanks for purchasing my book. I hope you enjoyed it. Apply my suggestions in your daily lives, and I'm sure you'll notice a change.

Keep on the "lookout" for my upcoming release, *A Better Crop of Folks*. It will soon be at your local bookstore.

Since your honest input will help to bring about my current release, parts of the proceeds will go to support the C.R.O.P. Scholarship Fund (Citizens Reaching Out to People) . . . a scholarship to assist the children of single parents.

Again, thanks a bunch! Together, we can make a difference.

*— Brittian Wilder III*

## For More Information

If you would like to have book author/lecturer Brittian Wilder III as a guest speaker for your organization or show, or catch the next available city on his international "For Women Only" promotional tour, please give us a call 24 hours a day, 7 days a week at: (800) 938-1788, Fax (310) 274-7588 or write:

>Winthrop and Collins, PC and Management
>269 S. Beverly Dr., #133
>Beverly Hills, California 90212

For a personal message from the author, call: (770) 281-4585.

If "Getting and Keeping Your Mate Trained, Whipped, Faithful, and on a Leash" is not available at your bookstore or through your distributor, call us 24 hours a day, 7 days a week at: (800) 938-1218

**GALLERY PUBLISHING**

# About the Author

Author/lecturer Brittian Wilder III is a popular talk show host and former writer and producer for the popular and award-winning, nationally syndicated radio show "Coast to Coast Top Twenty," hosted by Doug Steele and heard around the world.

The author is a graduate of the University of Alabama in Tuscaloosa and was born in Aliceville, Alabama. He is currently single and resides in Atlanta, Georgia.